NATIONAL
GEOGRAPHIC

GUIDE TO

NATIONAL

PARKS OF THE

UNITED

STATES

JOURNAL

NATIONAL GEOGRAPHIC

WASHINGTON, D.C.

THIS JOURNAL BELONGS TO:

_____

_____

_____

| CONTENTS

Map of the National Parks of the United States 4

THE NATIONAL PARKS

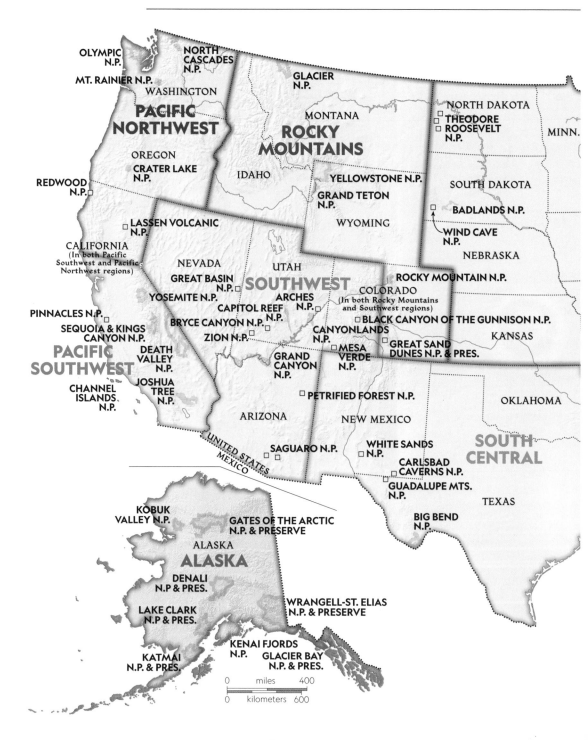

OLYMPIC N.P.

NORTH CASCADES N.P.

MT. RAINIER N.P.

GLACIER N.P.

WASHINGTON

NORTH DAKOTA

THEODORE ROOSEVELT N.P.

MINN.

PACIFIC NORTHWEST

MONTANA

ROCKY MOUNTAINS

OREGON

CRATER LAKE N.P.

IDAHO

SOUTH DAKOTA

REDWOOD N.P.

YELLOWSTONE N.P.

GRAND TETON N.P.

BADLANDS N.P.

WIND CAVE N.P.

WYOMING

LASSEN VOLCANIC N.P.

NEBRASKA

CALIFORNIA
(In both Pacific Southwest and Pacific Northwest regions)

NEVADA

UTAH

SOUTHWEST

ROCKY MOUNTAIN N.P.

GREAT BASIN N.P.

COLORADO
(In both Rocky Mountains and Southwest regions)

YOSEMITE N.P.

ARCHES N.P.

PINNACLES N.P.

CAPITOL REEF N.P.

BLACK CANYON OF THE GUNNISON N.P.

KANSAS

SEQUOIA & KINGS CANYON N.P.

BRYCE CANYON N.P.

CANYONLANDS N.P.

GREAT SAND DUNES N.P. & PRES.

PACIFIC SOUTHWEST

ZION N.P.

MESA VERDE N.P.

DEATH VALLEY N.P.

GRAND CANYON N.P.

CHANNEL ISLANDS N.P.

JOSHUA TREE N.P.

PETRIFIED FOREST N.P.

OKLAHOMA

ARIZONA

NEW MEXICO

UNITED STATES MEXICO

SAGUARO N.P.

WHITE SANDS N.P.

SOUTH CENTRAL

CARLSBAD CAVERNS N.P.

GUADALUPE MTS. N.P.

TEXAS

KOBUK VALLEY N.P.

GATES OF THE ARCTIC N.P. & PRESERVE

BIG BEND N.P.

ALASKA

ALASKA

DENALI N.P & PRES.

WRANGELL-ST. ELIAS N.P. & PRESERVE

LAKE CLARK N.P & PRES.

KENAI FJORDS N.P.

GLACIER BAY N.P. & PRES.

KATMAI N.P. & PRES.

0   miles   400

0   kilometers   600

OF THE UNITED STATES

VOYAGEURS N.P.

ISLE ROYALE N.P.

MAINE

ACADIA N.P.

CANADA
U.S.

VT.

N.H.

NEW YORK

MASS.

RHODE ISLAND

CONNECTICUT

N.J.

WISCONSIN

MICHIGAN

MIDWEST

IOWA

INDIANA DUNES N.P.

CUYAHOGA VALLEY N.P.

PENNSYLVANIA

MD.

DELAWARE

ILLINOIS

INDIANA

OHIO

W. VA.

SHENANDOAH N.P.

MISSOURI

NEW RIVER GORGE N.P. & PRES.

VIRGINIA

EAST

GATEWAY ARCH N.P.

KENTUCKY

MAMMOTH CAVE N.P.

N.C.

ARKANSAS

TENNESSEE

GREAT SMOKY MTS. N.P.

HOT SPRINGS N.P.

S.C.

CONGAREE N.P.

MISS.

ALABAMA

GEORGIA

LOUISIANA

FLORIDA

| miles | 0 | 400 |
| kilometers | 0 | 600 |

ALASKA (U.S.)

U.S. VIRGIN ISLANDS N.P. (EAST)

HAWAI'I (U.S.)

PACIFIC OCEAN

NATIONAL PARK OF AMERICAN SAMOA (PACIFIC SOUTHWEST)

HAWAI'I

PACIFIC SOUTHWEST

HALEAKALĀ N.P.

BISCAYNE N.P.

EVERGLADES N.P.

DRY TORTUGAS N.P.

| miles | 0 | 200 |
| kilometers | 0 | 300 |

HAWAI'I VOLCANOES N.P.

U.S. REGIONS

- East
- Midwest
- South Central
- Southwest
- Rocky Mountains
- Pacific Southwest
- Pacific Northwest
- Alaska

ACADIA

MAINE

VISITORS CENTERS: Hulls Cove Visitor Center **I** Bar Harbor Chamber of Commerce Visitor Center **I** Sieur de Monts Nature Center

WHEN TO GO: Late June and September offer pleasant temperatures and fewer crowds. Expect peak foliage in mid-October and high traffic in July and August. Park facilities are closed late October through April/May.

LODGING: Six campgrounds (tents, RVs) **I** Acadia Wilderness Lodge **I** Emery's Cottages on the Shore **I** Isleview Motel & Cottages **I** Rose Eden Cottages **I** Edgewater Motel, Cottages & Suites **I** Woodland Park Cottages **I** Tide Watch Cabins

---

HIKES:

Summit Hikes: Gorham Mountain Loop **I** Beehive Loop **I** Cadillac South Ridge Trail **I** Jordan Cliffs Loop **I** Beachcroft Path **I** Gorge Path **I** Beech Mountain South Ridge Loop **I** Flying Mountain Loop **I** Beech Mountain Trail **I** Precipice Loop **I** Giant Slide Loop **I** Norumbega Mountain Loop **I** Bubbles Nubble Loop **I** Pemetic South Ridge **I** Schiff Path **I** The Bubbles **I** Western Mountain Loop **I** Pemetic Mountain Loop **I** Emery Path **I** Homans Path

Coastal Hikes: Great Head Trail **I** Ship Harbor Trail **I** Bar Island Trail **I** Ocean Path Trail **I** Wonderland Trail **I** Schoodic Peninsula Trails **I** Compass Harbor Trail

Forest Hikes: Great Head Trail **I** Jordan Cliffs Loop **I** Jesup Path and Hemlock Path Loop **I** Hadlock Ponds Loop **I** Kurt Diederichs Climb **I** Homans Path **I** Jordan Pond Path **I** Witch Hole Pond Loop **I** Western Mountain Loop

ACTIVITIES:

Atlantic Climbing School **I** Bar Harbor Whale Watch Company cruise **I** Bass Harbor Head Light Station **I** Islesford Historical Museum **I** Lulu Lobster Boat ride **I** Rockefeller Hall **I** Sea Princess scenic nature cruises

WILDLIFE SPOTTING:

Bats **I** Beavers **I** Eagles **I** Foxes **I** Harbor porpoises **I** Harbor seals **I** Hawks **I** Loons **I** Mink **I** Peregrine falcons **I** Snowy owls **I** Vireos **I** Warblers **I** White-tailed deer

---

DATE VISITED:

WEATHER:

WHERE I WENT:

WHERE I STAYED:

WHO I WENT WITH:

FAVORITE MOMENT:

WHAT I'D RECOMMEND:

TIPS TO FRIENDS/ FAMILY:

WHAT I WISH I KNEW BEFORE GOING:

WHAT WAS THE FIRST THING I NOTICED WHEN I ARRIVED?

MY FAVORITE PART OF THE VISIT WAS . . .

HOW I SPENT MY TIME THERE:

WHAT WOULD I DO IF I GO BACK?

WHAT IS SOMETHING NEW I LEARNED?

MY TOP THREE FAVORITE ACTIVITIES WERE . . .

1.

2.

3

MY TRIP WAS

JAN   FEB   MAR   APR   MAY   JUN   JUL   AUG   SEP   OCT   NOV   DEC
1 2 3 4 5 6 7 8 9 10 11 12 13 14 15 16 17 18 19 20 21 22 23 24 25 26 27 28 29 30 31

....

....

....

....

....

....

....

....

....

....

....

....

....

....

....

....

....

....

....

....

....

....

....

BISCAYNE

FLORIDA

VISITORS CENTER: Dante Fascell Visitor Center

WHEN TO GO: December through April is the most popular time, with moderate temperatures and fewer mosquitoes. Water is the most calm and clear for snorkeling in the summer.

LODGING: Two campgrounds (tents)

ACTIVITIES:
Almost 95 percent of Biscayne National Park is underwater, so most of your activities will be on or below the water.
Boca Chita Key Heritage Cruise from Coconut Grove I Dante Fascell Visitor Center Gallery I Heritage of Biscayne Cruise I Snorkeling I Kayaking the Mangroves I Sails and Trails: Camp, Paddle, Sail, and Hike Island Trails I Paddling clear, calm waters on a Jones Lagoon Eco-Adventure I Deering Estate Boca Chita Key Cruise I Deering Estate Lighthouses Boat Cruise I Kayaking the Seagrasses of Stiltsville I Park After Dark Evening Sunset Bay Cruise

WILDLIFE SPOTTING:
American crocodiles I American eels I Atlantic blue marlins I Bermuda chub I Blue angelfish I Brown pelicans I Great barracuda I Manatees I Pompano dolphinfish I Porkfish I Schaus' swallowtail butterflies I Sea turtles I Wood storks

DATE VISITED:

WEATHER:

WHERE I WENT:

WHERE I STAYED:

WHO I WENT WITH:

FAVORITE MOMENT:

WHAT I'D RECOMMEND:

TIPS TO FRIENDS/ FAMILY:

WHAT I WISH I KNEW BEFORE GOING:

WHAT WAS THE FIRST THING I NOTICED WHEN I ARRIVED?

MY FAVORITE PART OF THE VISIT WAS . . .

HOW I SPENT MY TIME THERE:

WHAT WOULD I DO IF I GO BACK?

WHAT IS SOMETHING NEW I LEARNED?

MY TOP THREE FAVORITE ACTIVITIES WERE . . .

1.

2.

3

MY TRIP WAS

/10

JAN   FEB   MAR   APR   MAY   JUN   JUL   AUG   SEP   OCT   NOV   DEC
1 2 3 4 5 6 7 8 9 10 11 12 13 14 15 16 17 18 19 20 21 22 23 24 25 26 27 28 29 30 31

CONGAREE

SOUTH CAROLINA

VISITORS CENTER: Harry Hampton Visitor Center

WHEN TO GO: Congaree is most pleasant in the spring and fall, which coincides with bird migration season. Summer is often hot and humid, while bare trees afford longer views in the winter months.

LODGING: Two camp-grounds (tents)

- **HIKES:**

Easy: Bluff Trail I Boardwalk Loop Trail I Sims Trail I Bates Ferry Trail I Longleaf Trail I Firefly Trail
Moderate: Congaree River Blue Trail I Weston Lake Loop I Fork Swamp Trail
Difficult: Oakridge Trail I River Trail I Kingsnake Trail

- **WILDLIFE SPOTTING:**

Alligators I Bobcats I Brown water snakes I Fireflies I Owls I Prothonotary warblers I Red-cockaded woodpeckers I River otters I Skinks I Snapping turtles I White-tailed deer I Wild boars I Woodpeckers

- **ACTIVITIES:**

Annual Christmas Bird Count I Cedar Creek Canoe Trail I Ranger-led hikes I Synchronous Fireflies Viewing Event I Fishing

---

DATE VISITED:

WEATHER:

WHERE I WENT:

WHERE I STAYED:

WHO I WENT WITH:

FAVORITE MOMENT:

WHAT I'D RECOMMEND:

TIPS TO FRIENDS/ FAMILY:

WHAT I WISH I KNEW BEFORE GOING:

WHAT WAS THE FIRST THING I NOTICED WHEN I ARRIVED?

MY FAVORITE PART OF THE VISIT WAS . . .

HOW I SPENT MY TIME THERE:

WHAT WOULD I DO IF I GO BACK?

WHAT IS SOMETHING NEW I LEARNED?

MY TOP THREE FAVORITE ACTIVITIES WERE . . .

1.

2.

3

MY TRIP WAS

/10

JAN   FEB   MAR   APR   MAY   JUN   JUL   AUG   SEP   OCT   NOV   DEC
1 2 3 4 5 6 7 8 9 10 11 12 13 14 15 16 17 18 19 20 21 22 23 24 25 26 27 28 29 30 31

....

....

....

....

....

....

....

....

....

....

....

....

....

....

....

....

....

....

....

....

....

....

....

....

DRY TORTUGAS

FLORIDA

 **VISITORS CENTERS:** Fort Jefferson Visitor Center I Florida Keys Eco-Discovery Center

WHEN TO GO: The park can be visited year-round but only by boat or seaplane. November through April have cooler temperatures, whereas May through October bring warmer weather. Hurricanes can strike June through November.

LODGING: One campground (tents)

HIKES:
Fort Jefferson Loop I Bush Key Trail

ACTIVITIES:
Water vessel permits are required for all water activities.
Bird-watching tours I Dive excursions around the Keys I Guided ferry tour of Garden Key I Loggerhead Key kayaking (individuals must bring required equipment) I Paddleboarding throughout the Keys (individuals must bring required equipment) I Private charter boating around the Keys I

Snorkeling on self-guided tours along Fort Jefferson's moat wall I Snorkeling Garden Key I Snorkeling Windjammer wreck I Stargazing excursions I Touring Fort Jefferson

WILDLIFE SPOTTING:
Amberjacks I Barracuda I Butterfly fish I Goliath groupers I Gray angelfish I Green sea turtles I Hawksbill sea turtles I Lobsters I Loggerhead sea turtles I Magnificent frigatebirds I Moon jellyfish I Nurse sharks I Red hinds I Sea anemones I Sergeant majors I Staghorn coral I Stoplight parrotfish I Tarpons I Wahoo I White-tailed tropicbirds

DATE VISITED:

WEATHER:

WHERE I WENT:

WHERE I STAYED:

WHO I WENT WITH:

FAVORITE MOMENT:

WHAT I'D RECOMMEND:

TIPS TO FRIENDS/ FAMILY:

WHAT I WISH I KNEW BEFORE GOING:

WHAT WAS THE FIRST THING I NOTICED WHEN I ARRIVED?

MY FAVORITE PART OF THE VISIT WAS . . .

HOW I SPENT MY TIME THERE:

WHAT WOULD I DO IF I GO BACK?

WHAT IS SOMETHING NEW I LEARNED?

MY TOP THREE FAVORITE ACTIVITIES WERE . . .

1.

2.

3

MY TRIP WAS

/10

JAN   FEB   MAR   APR   MAY   JUN   JUL   AUG   SEP   OCT   NOV   DEC
1   2   3   4   5   6   7   8   9   10   11   12   13   14   15   16   17   18   19   20   21   22   23   24   25   26   27   28   29   30   31

....

....

....

....

....

....

....

....

....

....

....

....

....

....

....

....

....

....

....

....

EVERGLADES

FLORIDA

VISITORS CENTERS: Ernest F. Coe Visitor Center I Flamingo Visitor Center I Gulf Coast Visitor Center I Shark Valley Visitor Center

WHEN TO GO: There are two seasons: a wet season and a dry season. Dry season is generally more pleasant with more tours and activities, but it's also more crowded.

LODGING: Three campgrounds (tents)

HIKES:
Pine Island Trails: Anhinga Trail I Gumbo Limbo Trail I Mahogany Hammock Trail I Pahayokee Overlook I Pineland Trail
Flamingo Trails: Bear Lake Trail I Christian Point Trail I Coastal Prairie Trail I Eco Pond Trail I Guy Bradley Trail I Nine Mile Pond Canoe Trail I Rowdy Bend Trail I Snake Bight Trail I West Lake Trail
Shark Valley Trails: Bobcat Boardwalk I Otter Cave Hammock I Tamiami Trail
Gulf Coast Trails: Halfway Creek and Loop Trails I Loop Road Scenic Drive I Sandfly Island Hiking Trail I Turner River Paddling Trail

ACTIVITIES:
Bird-watching I Geocaching I Guided boat tours in the Gulf Coast area I Guided tour of Tram Road I Hells Bay Canoe Trail I Narrated boat tour at Buttonwood Canal I Paddleboarding/kayaking the Gulf Coast area I Ranger-led programs I Wilderness Waterway

WILDLIFE SPOTTING:
Alligators I Anhingas I Bald eagles I Bottlenose dolphins I Brown pelicans I Egrets I Flamingos I Florida panthers I Great blue herons I Manatees I Mangrove cuckoos I Ospreys I Roseate spoonbills I Snail kites I Turtles I White-crowned pigeons I Zebra longwing butterflies

DATE VISITED:

WEATHER:

WHERE I WENT:

WHERE I STAYED:

WHO I WENT WITH:

FAVORITE MOMENT:

WHAT I'D RECOMMEND:

TIPS TO FRIENDS/ FAMILY:

WHAT I WISH I KNEW BEFORE GOING:

WHAT WAS THE FIRST THING I NOTICED WHEN I ARRIVED?

MY FAVORITE PART OF THE VISIT WAS . . .

HOW I SPENT MY TIME THERE:

WHAT WOULD I DO IF I GO BACK?

WHAT IS SOMETHING NEW I LEARNED?

MY TOP THREE FAVORITE ACTIVITIES WERE . . .

1.

2.

3

MY TRIP WAS

/10

JAN   FEB   MAR   APR   MAY   JUN   JUL   AUG   SEP   OCT   NOV   DEC
1 2 3 4 5 6 7 8 9 10 11 12 13 14 15 16 17 18 19 20 21 22 23 24 25 26 27 28 29 30 31

....

....

....

....

....

....

....

....

....

....

....

....

....

....

....

....

....

....

....

....

....

....

GREAT SMOKY MOUNTAINS

NORTH CAROLINA & TENNESSEE

 VISITORS CENTERS: Cades Cove Visitor Center I Oconaluftee Visitor Center I Sugarlands Visitor Center

WHEN TO GO: The park is open year-round; however, summer and October weekends are the most crowded, and sometimes Clingmans Dome Road and Newfound Gap may be closed in the winter.

LODGING: Ten campgrounds (tents, RVs, horses) I LeConte Lodge

---

HIKES:

Easy: Portion of the Appalachian Trail I Cades Cove Loop Road I Cove Hardwoods Nature Trail I Deep Creek Loop Trail I Oconaluftee River Trail I Porters Creek Trail I Roaring Fork Motor Nature Trail

Moderate: Abrams Falls Trail I Appalachian Trail to Charlies Bunion I Rainbow Falls Trail

Difficult: Alum Cave Trail I Chimney Tops Trail I Ramsey Cascades Trail

ACTIVITIES:

Spring Wildflower Pilgrimage I Cable Mill tour I Elijah Oliver Place tour I Fishing I Guided horseback riding tours I Great Smoky Mountains Heritage Center I Mountain Farm Museum

WILDLIFE SPOTTING:

Barred owls I Black bears I Coyotes I Crayfish I Eastern box turtles I Elk I Gray squirrels I Raccoons I Salamanders I White-tailed deer I Wild turkeys I Woodchucks

---

DATE VISITED:

WEATHER:

WHERE I WENT:

WHERE I STAYED:

WHO I WENT WITH:

FAVORITE MOMENT:

WHAT I'D RECOMMEND:

TIPS TO FRIENDS/ FAMILY:

WHAT I WISH I KNEW BEFORE GOING:

WHAT WAS THE FIRST THING I NOTICED WHEN I ARRIVED?

MY FAVORITE PART OF THE VISIT WAS . . .

HOW I SPENT MY TIME THERE:

WHAT WOULD I DO IF I GO BACK?

WHAT IS SOMETHING NEW I LEARNED?

MY TOP THREE FAVORITE ACTIVITIES WERE . . .

1.

2.

3

MY TRIP WAS

/10

JAN   FEB   MAR   APR   MAY   JUN   JUL   AUG   SEP   OCT   NOV   DEC
1 2 3 4 5 6 7 8 9 10 11 12 13 14 15 16 17 18 19 20 21 22 23 24 25 26 27 28 29 30 31

MAMMOTH CAVE

KENTUCKY

VISITORS CENTER: Mammoth Cave Visitor Center

WHEN TO GO: The cave is open all year long, but tours are offered more regularly in the summer months. All activities are best Memorial Day through Labor Day.

LODGING: Three campgrounds (tents, RVs) I The Lodge at Mammoth Cave

- **HIKES:**
Big Hollow Trail I Cedar Sink Trail I Echo River Spring Trail I River Styx Spring Trail I Sand Cave Trail I Sloan's Crossing Pond Trail I White Oak Trail

- **CAVE TOURS:**
Easy: Focus on Frozen Niagara Photo Tour (only for photographers) I Frozen Niagara Tour I Trog Tour (ages 8–12)
Moderate: Cleveland Avenue Tour I Domes & Dripstones Tour I Gothic Avenue Tour I Great Onyx Lantern Tour (ages 6+) I Historic Tour I Star Chamber Lantern Tour (ages 6+)

Difficult: Grand Avenue Tour (ages 6+) I Introduction to Caving Tour (ages 10+) I Violet City Lantern Tour (ages 6+) I Wild Cave Tour (ages 16+)

- **ACTIVITIES:**
Fishing the Green River I Canoeing/kayaking/boating the Green River I Horseback riding tours I Mountain biking I Stargazing with rangers I Ranger-led programs

- **WILDLIFE SPOTTING:**
Bluegills I Catfish I Smallmouth bass

DATE VISITED:

WEATHER:

WHERE I WENT:

WHERE I STAYED:

WHO I WENT WITH:

FAVORITE MOMENT:

WHAT I'D RECOMMEND:

TIPS TO FRIENDS/ FAMILY:

WHAT I WISH I KNEW BEFORE GOING:

WHAT WAS THE FIRST THING I NOTICED WHEN I ARRIVED?

MY FAVORITE PART
OF THE VISIT WAS . . .

HOW I SPENT MY TIME THERE:

WHAT WOULD I DO IF I GO BACK?

WHAT IS SOMETHING
NEW I LEARNED?

MY TOP THREE FAVORITE ACTIVITIES WERE . . .

1.

2.

3

MY TRIP
WAS

/10

NEW RIVER GORGE

WEST VIRGINIA

VISITORS CENTERS: Canyon Rim Visitor Center **I** Grandview Visitor Center **I** Sandstone Visitor Center **I** Thurmond Depot Visitor Center

WHEN TO GO: April through October are the best months to visit the park; temperatures are nice and activities are abundant.

LODGING: Nine campgrounds (tents, small RVs, RVs)

HIKES:

Easy: Big Buck Trail **I** Burnwood Trail **I** Butcher Branch Trail **I** Canyon Rim Boardwalk **I** Clovis Trail **I** Endless Wall Trail **I** Long Point Trail **I** Park Loop Trail **I** Sandstone Falls Boardwalk **I** Timber Ridge Trail **I** Tunnel Trail

Moderate: Big Branch Trail **I** Brooklyn Mine Trail **I** Castle Rock Trail **I** The Face Trail **I** Fayetteville Trail **I** Headhouse Trail **I** Kates Plateau Trail **I** Little Laurel Trail **I** Polls Plateau Trail **I** Rend Trail **I** Stone Cliff Trail **I** Thurmond-Southside Trail

Difficult: Gwinn Ridge Trail **I** Kaymoor Miners Trail **I** Conveyor Trail

ACTIVITIES:

Babcock State Park **I** Mountain biking **I** Climbing **I** Grandview Main Overlook **I** Hawks Nest State Park **I** New River Gorge Bridge Walk **I** New River Gorge Scenic Drive **I** Ranger-led programs **I** Visiting historic town of Thurmond **I** White-water rafting on New River

WILDLIFE SPOTTING:

Allegheny wood rats **I** Bald eagles **I** Beavers **I** Chipmunks **I** Coyotes **I** Eastern small-footed bats **I** Gray foxes **I** Gray squirrels **I** Groundhogs **I** Indiana bats **I** Mink **I** Peregrine falcons **I** Raccoons **I** Red foxes **I** River otters **I** Ruby-throated hummingbirds **I** Virginia big-eared bats **I** White-tailed deer

---

DATE VISITED:

WEATHER:

WHERE I WENT:

WHERE I STAYED:

WHO I WENT WITH:

FAVORITE MOMENT:

WHAT I'D RECOMMEND:

TIPS TO FRIENDS/ FAMILY:

WHAT I WISH I KNEW BEFORE GOING:

WHAT WAS THE FIRST THING I NOTICED WHEN I ARRIVED?

MY FAVORITE PART OF THE VISIT WAS . . .

HOW I SPENT MY TIME THERE:

WHAT WOULD I DO IF I GO BACK?

WHAT IS SOMETHING NEW I LEARNED?

MY TOP THREE FAVORITE ACTIVITIES WERE . . .

1.

2.

3

MY TRIP WAS

/10

JAN	FEB	MAR	APR	MAY	JUN	JUL	AUG	SEP	OCT	NOV	DEC
1 2 3	4 5 6	7 8 9	10 11 12	13 14 15	16 17	18 19 20	21 22	23 24	25 26 27	28 29	30 31

SHENANDOAH

VIRGINIA

 VISITORS CENTERS: Dickey Ridge Visitor Center I Harry F. Byrd, Sr. Visitor Center

WHEN TO GO: Traveling during the week in peak seasons is recommended to avoid weekend crowds. Lodging books up quickly for summer and in October for the fall foliage. Most facilities are closed for winter until March.

LODGING: Five campgrounds (tents, RVs) I Big Meadows Lodge I Lewis Mountain Cabins I Potomac Appalachian Trail Club I Skyland Lodging

---

HIKES:

Easy: Blackrock Summit I Dickey Ridge Trail I Fox Hollow Trail I Limberlost Trail I Mill Prong Trail I Snead Farm Loop Trail I Stony Man Trail I Traces Trail

Moderate: Frazier Discovery Trail I Hazel River Falls I Jones Run Falls Trail I Marys Rock Summit I Overall Run Falls I Rose River Trail I South River Overlook I Stony Man Horse Trail I Tuscarora-Overall Run Trail

Difficult: Bearfence Rock Scramble I Cedar Run-Whiteoak Circuit I Compton Peak I Dark Hollow Falls Trail I Hawksbill Summit Trail I Little Devils Stairs Trail I Old Rag Circuit

ACTIVITIES:

Biking I Cruising Skyline Drive I Fishing I Motorcoach Group Tours I Ranger-guided programs I Rapidan Camp Tours I Sky Meadows State Park I Stargazing

WILDLIFE SPOTTING:

American eels I Barred owls I Big brown bats I Black bears I Bobcats I Brook trout I Carolina chickadees I Coyotes I Hawks I Moles I Shenandoah salamanders I Shrews I Spotted skunks I Voles I White-tailed deer I Wild turkeys

---

DATE VISITED:

WEATHER:

WHERE I WENT:

WHERE I STAYED:

WHO I WENT WITH:

FAVORITE MOMENT:

WHAT I'D RECOMMEND:

TIPS TO FRIENDS/ FAMILY:

WHAT I WISH I KNEW BEFORE GOING:

WHAT WAS THE FIRST THING I NOTICED WHEN I ARRIVED?

MY FAVORITE PART OF THE VISIT WAS . . .

HOW I SPENT MY TIME THERE:

WHAT WOULD I DO IF I GO BACK?

WHAT IS SOMETHING NEW I LEARNED?

MY TOP THREE FAVORITE ACTIVITIES WERE . . .

1.

2.

3

MY TRIP WAS

/10

JAN   FEB   MAR   APR   MAY   JUN   JUL   AUG   SEP   OCT   NOV   DEC
1 2 3 4 5 6 7 8 9 10 11 12 13 14 15 16 17 18 19 20 21 22 23 24 25 26 27 28 29 30 31

....

....

....

....

....

....

....

....

....

....

....

....

....

....

....

....

....

....

....

....

....

....

....

VIRGIN ISLANDS

U.S. VIRGIN ISLANDS

VISITORS CENTER: Cruz Bay Visitor Center

WHEN TO GO: The weather is pleasant year-round. November and December are the rainiest months, February through April are the driest, and hurricanes may occur between August and November.

LODGING (ST. JOHN): One campground (tents, cabins) I Westin St. John Resort Villas **(ST. THOMAS):** Bolongo Bay Beach Resort I Emerald Beach Resort I Secret Harbour Beach Resort I Secret Haven Villa I Sea Ya Round Villa I The Ritz-Carlton, St. Thomas

- **HIKES:**
Easy: Cinnamon Bay Nature Loop I Francis Bay Trail I Leinster Bay Trail I Lind Point Trail I Francis Bay Trail I Salt Pond Bay Trail I Tektite Trail I Yawzi Point Trail
Moderate: Johnny Horn Trail I L'Esperance Trail I Reef Bay Trail I Ram Head Trail

- **ACTIVITIES:**
Annaberg Sugar Plantation tour I Canoeing/kayaking Princess Bay I Exploring Catherineberg Sugar Mill Ruins I Visiting Coral Bay's cafés and shops I Guided Reef Bay Trail tours I Trunk Bay Underwater Snorkel Trail I Snorkeling/diving at Cow and Calf Rocks I Snorkeling Waterlemon Cay I Spotting sea turtles at Francis Bay I Sunbathing at Trunk Bay Beach I Visiting family-friendly Maho Beach

- **WILDLIFE SPOTTING:**
Bananaquits I Barracuda I Bats I Carib hummingbirds I Dolphins I Donkeys I Goats I Green turtles I Hermit crabs I Iguanas I Mongooses I Parrotfish I Pearly-eyed thrashers I Pelicans I Spotted eagle rays I Tarpons I Whales

---

DATE VISITED:

WEATHER:

WHERE I WENT:

WHERE I STAYED:

WHO I WENT WITH:

FAVORITE MOMENT:

WHAT I'D RECOMMEND:

TIPS TO FRIENDS/ FAMILY:

WHAT I WISH I KNEW BEFORE GOING:

WHAT WAS THE FIRST THING I NOTICED WHEN I ARRIVED?

MY FAVORITE PART OF THE VISIT WAS . . .

HOW I SPENT MY TIME THERE:

WHAT WOULD I DO IF I GO BACK?

WHAT IS SOMETHING NEW I LEARNED?

MY TOP THREE FAVORITE ACTIVITIES WERE . . .

1.

2.

3

MY TRIP WAS

/10

JAN	FEB	MAR	APR	MAY	JUN	JUL	AUG	SEP	OCT	NOV	DEC
1 2 3	4 5 6	7 8 9	10 11 12	13 14 15	16 17 18	19 20	21 22	23 24	25 26 27	28 29	30 31

....

....

....

....

....

....

....

....

....

....

....

....

....

....

....

....

....

....

....

....

....

....

....

BADLANDS

SOUTH DAKOTA

VISITORS CENTERS: Ben Reifel Visitor Center **I** White River Visitor Center

WHEN TO GO: The largest crowds come during the summer months, when the weather is extremely hot, whereas spring and fall are more moderate. Even winter is beautiful, but the weather forecast must be watched.

LODGING: Backcountry camping (no permit required) **I** One campground (tents, RVs) **I** Cedar Pass Lodge and Campground

---

HIKES:

Easy: Big Badlands Overlook I Cliff Shelf Nature Trail I Door Trail I Fossil Exhibit Trail I Sage Creek Trail I Window Trail I Medicine Root Loop

Moderate: Burns Basin Overlook I Castle Trail I Cedar Butte Trail I Notch Trail I Saddle Pass Trail I Sheep Mountain Table Road I Sage Creek Wilderness Loop

Difficult: Sage Creek Loop

ACTIVITIES:

Badlands Astronomy Festival I Biking the Badlands I Driving Badlands Loop Road I Driving around the South Unit I Driving Sage Creek Rim Road I Fossil Preparation Lab I Guided ranger tours I Horseback riding I Night sky viewing excursions

WILDLIFE SPOTTING:

Bighorn sheep I Bison I Black-footed ferrets I Burrowing owls I Coyotes I Deer I Prairie dogs I Prairie rattlesnakes I Pronghorn I Snakes I Swift foxes I Western meadowlarks

---

DATE VISITED:

WEATHER:

WHERE I WENT:

WHERE I STAYED:

WHO I WENT WITH:

FAVORITE MOMENT:

WHAT I'D RECOMMEND:

TIPS TO FRIENDS/ FAMILY:

WHAT I WISH I KNEW BEFORE GOING:

WHAT WAS THE FIRST THING I NOTICED WHEN I ARRIVED?

MY FAVORITE PART OF THE VISIT WAS . . .

HOW I SPENT MY TIME THERE:

WHAT WOULD I DO IF I GO BACK?

WHAT IS SOMETHING NEW I LEARNED?

MY TOP THREE FAVORITE ACTIVITIES WERE . . .

1.

2.

3

MY TRIP WAS

/10

JAN   FEB   MAR   APR   MAY   JUN   JUL   AUG   SEP   OCT   NOV   DEC
1 2 3 4 5 6 7 8 9 10 11 12 13 14 15 16 17 18 19 20 21 22 23 24 25 26 27 28 29 30 31

....

....

....

....

....

....

....

....

....

....

....

....

....

....

....

....

....

....

....

....

....

....

CUYAHOGA VALLEY

OHIO

 VISITORS CENTER: Boston Mill Visitor Center

WHEN TO GO: Late spring through fall is best for hiking and seeing colorful foliage, while winter is popular for cross-country skiing and sledding.

LODGING: Inn at Brandywine Falls I Stanford House

HIKES:
Easy: Beaver Marsh I Brandywine Falls Loop I Bridal Veils Falls Overlook I Cuyahoga Valley Trail I Forest Point Trail I Haskell Run Trail I Hemlock Creek Trail I Kendall Lake Loop I Oak Hill Trail I Ohio & Erie Canal Towpath Trail I Perkins Trail I Pine Grove Trail I Plateau Trail I Tree Farm Trail
Moderate: Blue Hen Falls I Boston Run Trail I Brandywine Gorge Trail I Cuyahoga Valley Ledges Trail I Furnace Run I Lamb Loop I Old Carriage Trail I Riding Run Loop Trail I Salt Run I Tinker's Creek Gorge Scenic Overlook I Valley Bridle Trail I Wetmore Bridle Trail

ACTIVITIES:
Canal Exploration Center I Canalway questing I Cuyahoga Valley Scenic Railroad I Everett Covered Bridge I Hale Farm & Village I Horseback riding I Living history events on the Ohio & Erie Canal I Paddling/kayaking the Cuyahoga River I Sledding or cross-country skiing I Virginia Kendall Park I Visiting Peninsula village's shops and art galleries I Wildlife-watching at Beaver Marsh

WILDLIFE SPOTTING:
Bald eagles I Bats I Beavers I Blue herons I Canada warblers I Coyotes I Foxes I Hermit thrushes I Mink I Muskrats I Otters I Spotted turtles I Winter wrens I Woodchucks

---

DATE VISITED:

WEATHER:

WHERE I WENT:

WHERE I STAYED:

WHO I WENT WITH:

FAVORITE MOMENT:

WHAT I'D RECOMMEND:

TIPS TO FRIENDS/ FAMILY:

WHAT I WISH I KNEW BEFORE GOING:

WHAT WAS THE FIRST THING I NOTICED WHEN I ARRIVED?

MY FAVORITE PART OF THE VISIT WAS . . .

HOW I SPENT MY TIME THERE:

WHAT WOULD I DO IF I GO BACK?

WHAT IS SOMETHING NEW I LEARNED?

MY TOP THREE FAVORITE ACTIVITIES WERE . . .

1.

2.

3

MY TRIP WAS

/10

JAN   FEB   MAR   APR   MAY   JUN   JUL   AUG   SEP   OCT   NOV   DEC
1 2 3 4 5 6 7 8 9 10 11 12 13 14 15 16 17 18 19 20 21 22 23 24 25 26 27 28 29 30 31

GATEWAY ARCH

MISSOURI

 VISITORS CENTER: The Museum at the Gateway Arch

WHEN TO GO: The Gateway Arch, its museum, and Old Courthouse are open year-round, although steamboat cruises do not operate from December to March. There are shorter wait times for the tram outside of the busy summer season.

LODGING: The park has no lodging, but St. Louis has hotels and home rentals.

HIKES:
No hikes, but plentiful paths to stroll

ACTIVITIES:
Arch Bark canine-centered festival I Blues at the Arch Festival I Ice-skating at Kiener Plaza I Museum at the Gateway Arch I Old Courthouse tour I Old Rock House I Sightseeing

and riverboat cruises on the Mississippi River I Sunrise Yoga I Visiting the reflection ponds

WILDLIFE SPOTTING:
American goldfinches I American white pelicans I Bobolinks I Killdeer I Painted buntings I Purple finches I Raccoons I Rose-breasted grosbeaks I Ruby-throated hummingbirds I Squirrels I Yellow-headed blackbirds

DATE VISITED:

WEATHER:

WHERE I WENT:

WHERE I STAYED:

WHO I WENT WITH:

FAVORITE MOMENT:

WHAT I'D RECOMMEND:

TIPS TO FRIENDS/ FAMILY:

WHAT I WISH I KNEW BEFORE GOING:

WHAT WAS THE FIRST THING I NOTICED WHEN I ARRIVED?

MY FAVORITE PART OF THE VISIT WAS . . .

HOW I SPENT MY TIME THERE:

WHAT WOULD I DO IF I GO BACK?

WHAT IS SOMETHING NEW I LEARNED?

MY TOP THREE FAVORITE ACTIVITIES WERE . . .

1.

2.

3

MY TRIP WAS

INDIANA DUNES

INDIANA

VISITORS CENTER: Indiana Dunes Visitor Center

WHEN TO GO: Spring is best for wildflowers and bird-watching; summer is great for beachgoers; and fall is perfect for colorful hiking experiences.

LODGING: One campground (tents, RVs)

HIKES:

Easy: Bailly Homestead, Chellberg Farm, Little Calumet River, and Mnoké Prairie Trails I Calumet Dunes Trail I Great Marsh Trail I Heron Rookery Trail I Hobart Woodland Trail I Portage Lakefront and Riverwalk Trail

Moderate: Cowles Bog Trail I Dune Ridge Trail I Glenwood Dunes Trail I Paul H. Douglas Trail I Tolleston Dunes Trail I West Beach 3-Loop Trail

Difficult: Dune Succession Trail

ACTIVITIES:

Bailly Homestead I Chellberg Farmhouse I Biking I Bird-watching tours I Cross-country skiing and snowshoeing I Fishing the Little Calumet River I Geocaching I Horseback riding I Indiana Dunes Outdoor Adventure Festival I Maple Sugar Time Festival I Mount Baldy ranger-led program I Paul H. Douglas Center for Environmental Education I Pinhook Bog ranger-led tour I Swimming at West Beach

WILDLIFE SPOTTING:

Baltimore orioles I Bass I Beavers I Coyotes I Eastern chipmunks I Eastern cottontails I Eastern red bats I Karner blue butterflies I Meadow voles I Norway rats I Red foxes I Salmon I Six-lined racerunners I Southern flying squirrels I Tanagers I Thrushes I Trout I Warblers I White-tailed deer I Woodchucks

---

DATE VISITED:

WEATHER:

WHERE I WENT:

WHERE I STAYED:

WHO I WENT WITH:

FAVORITE MOMENT:

WHAT I'D RECOMMEND:

TIPS TO FRIENDS/ FAMILY:

WHAT I WISH I KNEW BEFORE GOING:

WHAT WAS THE FIRST THING I NOTICED WHEN I ARRIVED?

MY FAVORITE PART OF THE VISIT WAS . . .

HOW I SPENT MY TIME THERE:

WHAT WOULD I DO IF I GO BACK?

WHAT IS SOMETHING NEW I LEARNED?

MY TOP THREE FAVORITE ACTIVITIES WERE . . .

1.

2.

3

MY TRIP WAS

/10

JAN   FEB   MAR   APR   MAY   JUN   JUL   AUG   SEP   OCT   NOV   DEC
1 2 3   4 5 6   7 8 9   10 11 12   13 14 15   16 17 18   19 20   21 22   23 24   25 26 27   28 29   30 31

ISLE ROYALE

MICHIGAN

 VISITORS CENTERS: Houghton Visitor Center I Windigo Visitor Center I Rock Harbor Visitor Center

 **WHEN TO GO:** The park is open mid-April through October, but stormy conditions on Lake Superior in the spring can affect transportation to the island.

LODGING: Backcountry camping (permit required) I Rock Harbor Lodge I Windigo Camper Cabins

---

HIKES:

Easy: Daisy Farm Trail I Rainbow Cove Trail I Windigo Nature Trail

Moderate: Feldtmann Lake Trail I Feldtmann Ridge Trail I Grace Creek Overlook I Indian Portage Trail I Lookout Louise Trail I Mount Ojibway Trail I Raspberry Island Loop I Scoville Point via Stoll Trail I Suzy's Cave Trail I Tobin Harbor Trail I Mount Franklin Trail

Difficult: Feldtmann Lake Loop Trail I Greenstone Ridge Trail I Lane Cove Trail I Minong Ridge Trail

ACTIVITIES:

Backpacking I Boating to Raspberry Island I Canoeing Tobin Harbor I Kayaking over the wreck of the S.S. *America* I Guided boat trips to Edisen Fishery I Guided boat trips to Rock Harbor Lighthouse

WILDLIFE SPOTTING:

Bald eagles I Beavers I Foxes I Gray wolves I Loons I Moose I River otters I Sandhill cranes I Sharp-tailed grouse I Snowshoe hares I Western painted turtles

---

DATE VISITED:

WEATHER:

WHERE I WENT:

WHERE I STAYED:

WHO I WENT WITH:

FAVORITE MOMENT:

WHAT I'D RECOMMEND:

TIPS TO FRIENDS/ FAMILY:

WHAT I WISH I KNEW BEFORE GOING:

WHAT WAS THE FIRST THING I NOTICED WHEN I ARRIVED?

MY FAVORITE PART OF THE VISIT WAS . . .

HOW I SPENT MY TIME THERE:

WHAT WOULD I DO IF I GO BACK?

WHAT IS SOMETHING NEW I LEARNED?

MY TOP THREE FAVORITE ACTIVITIES WERE . . .

1.

2.

3

MY TRIP WAS

....

....

....

....

....

....

....

....

....

....

....

....

....

....

....

....

....

....

....

....

....

....

THEODORE ROOSEVELT

NORTH DAKOTA

 VISITORS CENTERS: Painted Canyon Visitor Center I South Unit Visitor Center I North Unit Visitor Center

WHEN TO GO: Summer is the busiest season, while fall brings colorful foliage and fewer people. In winter, parts of the park's roads may be closed.

LODGING: Three campgrounds (tents, RVs, horses)

HIKES:

Easy: Boicourt Overlook Trail I Little Mo Nature Trail I Painted Canyon Nature Trail I Skyline Vista I Wind Canyon Trail

Moderate: Buckhorn Trail I Coal Vein Trail I Caprock Coulee Nature Trail I Jones Creek Trail I Jones/Lower Talkington/Lower Paddock Loop I Lone Tree Spring Trail I Petrified Forest Trail I River Bend Overlook I Upper Talkington Loop Trail

Difficult: Achenbach Trail I Maah Daah Hey Trail

ACTIVITIES:

Cross Ranch State Park I Cruising the 36-mile Scenic Loop Drive I Elkhorn Ranch Unit I Lake Ilo National Wildlife Refuge I Little Missouri National Grassland I Lostwood National Wildlife Refuge I Maltese Cross Cabin I Peaceful Valley Ranch I Ranger-led walks or programs I Roadside prairie dog towns I Sully Creek State Park

WILDLIFE SPOTTING:

Badgers I Bighorn sheep I Bison I Black-tailed prairie dogs I Coyotes I Elk I Feral horses I Golden eagles I Great horned owls I Mules I Porcupines I Pronghorn I White-tailed deer

---

DATE VISITED:

WEATHER:

WHERE I WENT:

WHERE I STAYED:

WHO I WENT WITH:

FAVORITE MOMENT:

WHAT I'D RECOMMEND:

TIPS TO FRIENDS/ FAMILY:

WHAT I WISH I KNEW BEFORE GOING:

WHAT WAS THE FIRST THING I NOTICED WHEN I ARRIVED?

MY FAVORITE PART OF THE VISIT WAS . . .

HOW I SPENT MY TIME THERE:

WHAT WOULD I DO IF I GO BACK?

WHAT IS SOMETHING NEW I LEARNED?

MY TOP THREE FAVORITE ACTIVITIES WERE . . .

1.

2.

3

MY TRIP WAS

/10

JAN   FEB   MAR   APR   MAY   JUN   JUL   AUG   SEP   OCT   NOV   DEC
1 2 3 4 5 6 7 8 9 10 11 12 13 14 15 16 17 18 19 20 21 22 23 24 25 26 27 28 29 30 31

VOYAGEURS

MINNESOTA

 VISITORS CENTERS: Ash River Visitor Center **I** Kabetogama Lake Visitor Center **I** Rainy Lake Visitor Center

WHEN TO GO: The park's main season runs from mid-May to late September, with peak visitation around July 4. Many visitors enjoy mid-September for the smaller crowds. Winter offers many snow activities.

LODGING: All campsites require permits; primitive campsites are accessible via the Kab-Ash Trail; front-country and backcountry campsites can be reached by boat only **I** Kettle Falls Hotel

HIKES:

Easy: Anderson Bay Loop I Beaver Pond Overlook Trail I Echo Bay Trail I Ethno-botanical Garden I Kabetogama Lake Overlook Trail I Oberholtzer Trail I Rainy Lake Recreation Trail I Sullivan Bay Trail I Voyageurs Forest Overlook Trail
Moderate: Black Bay Beaver Pond Trail I Blind Ash Bay Trail I Kab-Ash Trail I Mukooda Trail
Difficult: Cruiser Lake Trail I Locator Lake Trail

ACTIVITIES:

Bushyhead Island I Discovery Cruise (boat tour) I Ellsworth Rock Gardens I Family canoe trip I Grand Tour (boat tour) I Kettle Falls I Kettle Falls Cruise (boat tour) I North Canoe Voyage I Starwatch Cruise (boat tour) I Watercraft rentals (including houseboats)

WILDLIFE SPOTTING:

American toads I Beavers I Black bears I Common snapping turtles I Eagles I Gray wolves I Loons I Moose I Muskrats I Otters I Owls I White-tailed deer I Wood frogs

DATE VISITED:

WEATHER:

WHERE I WENT:

WHERE I STAYED:

WHO I WENT WITH:

FAVORITE MOMENT:

WHAT I'D RECOMMEND:

TIPS TO FRIENDS/ FAMILY:

WHAT I WISH I KNEW BEFORE GOING:

WHAT WAS THE FIRST THING I NOTICED WHEN I ARRIVED?

MY FAVORITE PART OF THE VISIT WAS . . .

HOW I SPENT MY TIME THERE:

WHAT WOULD I DO IF I GO BACK?

WHAT IS SOMETHING NEW I LEARNED?

MY TOP THREE FAVORITE ACTIVITIES WERE . . .

1.

2.

3

MY TRIP WAS

/10

JAN   FEB   MAR   APR   MAY   JUN   JUL   AUG   SEP   OCT   NOV   DEC
1 2 3 4 5 6 7 8 9 10 11 12 13 14 15 16 17 18 19 20 21 22 23 24 25 26 27 28 29 30 31

WIND CAVE

SOUTH DAKOTA

 **VISITORS CENTER:** Wind Cave National Park Visitor Center

WHEN TO GO: Summer and early fall are the most popular seasons. Cave tours are on a first come, first served basis and summer can have longer wait times.

LODGING: One campground (tents)

- **HIKES:**
Easy: Cold Brook Canyon Trail I Elk Mountain Campground Loop I Prairie Vista Loop I Rankin Ridge Nature Trail I Wind Cave Canyon Trail
Moderate: Boland Ridge Trail I East Bison Flats Trail I Elk Mountain Trail I Lookout Point Trail
Difficult: Highland Creek Trail to Centennial Loop Trail

- **CAVE TOURS:**
Accessibility Tour I Candlelight Tour I Fairgrounds Tour I Garden of Eden Tour I Natural Entrance Tour I Wild Cave Tour

- **ACTIVITIES:**
Elk bugling programs

- **WILDLIFE SPOTTING:**
Bison I Elk I Great horned owls I Mule deer I Northern flickers I Prairie dogs I Pronghorn I Sharp-tailed grouse I Western meadowlarks I White-tailed deer

DATE VISITED:

WEATHER:

WHERE I WENT:

WHERE I STAYED:

WHO I WENT WITH:

FAVORITE MOMENT:

WHAT I'D RECOMMEND:

TIPS TO FRIENDS/ FAMILY:

WHAT I WISH I KNEW BEFORE GOING:

WHAT WAS THE FIRST THING I NOTICED WHEN I ARRIVED?

MY FAVORITE PART OF THE VISIT WAS . . .

HOW I SPENT MY TIME THERE:

WHAT WOULD I DO IF I GO BACK?

WHAT IS SOMETHING NEW I LEARNED?

MY TOP THREE FAVORITE ACTIVITIES WERE . . .

1.

2.

3

MY TRIP WAS

/10

JAN	FEB	MAR	APR	MAY	JUN	JUL	AUG	SEP	OCT	NOV	DEC

1 2 3 4 5 6 7 8 9 10 11 12 13 14 15 16 17 18 19 20 21 22 23 24 25 26 27 28 29 30 31

....

....

....

....

....

....

....

....

....

....

....

....

....

....

....

....

....

....

....

....

BIG BEND

TEXAS

 VISITORS CENTERS: Castolon Visitor Center | Chisos Basin Visitor Center | Panther Junction Visitor Center | Persimmon Gap Visitor Center | Rio Grande Village Visitor Center

 **WHEN TO GO:** Temperatures are best fall through spring, while summer is extremely hot.

 **LODGING:** Backcountry camping (permit required) | Three campgrounds (tents, small RVs, RVs) | Chisos Mountains Lodge | Rio Grande Village RV Park

HIKES:

Easy: Big Bend Hot Springs Trail | Boquillas Canyon Trail | Chihuahuan Desert Nature Trail | Dog Canyon Trail | Lone Mountain Trail | Panther Path | Rio Grande Village Nature Trail | Window View Trail
Moderate: Chimneys Trail | Chisos Basin Loop Trail | Colima Trail | Grapevine Hills Trail | Lost Mine Trail | Mule Ears Spring Trail | Santa Elena Canyon Trail | Window Trail
Difficult: Blue Creek Trail | Boot Canyon Trail | Emory Peak | Pinnacles Trail | South Rim Trail

ACTIVITIES:

Bird-watching on the Rio Grande | Canoeing, floating, kayaking, rafting the Rio Grande (permit required) | Driving Old Maverick Road | Fossil spotting | Boquillas del Carmen, Mexico (passport required) | Homer Wilson Ranch | Hot springing | Sam Nail Ranch | Terlingua Abajo ruins

WILDLIFE SPOTTING:

Acorn woodpeckers | Bats | Beavers | Black bears | Carmen Mountain white-tailed deer | Colima warblers | Common black hawks | Gray hawks | Javelinas | Mexican jays | Mountain lions | Mule deer | Painted buntings | Scorpions | Vermilion flycatchers | Western tanagers

---

DATE VISITED:

WEATHER:

WHERE I WENT:

WHERE I STAYED:

WHO I WENT WITH:

FAVORITE MOMENT:

WHAT I'D RECOMMEND:

TIPS TO FRIENDS/FAMILY:

WHAT I WISH I KNEW BEFORE GOING:

WHAT WAS THE FIRST THING I NOTICED WHEN I ARRIVED?

MY FAVORITE PART OF THE VISIT WAS . . .

HOW I SPENT MY TIME THERE:

WHAT WOULD I DO IF I GO BACK?

WHAT IS SOMETHING NEW I LEARNED?

MY TOP THREE FAVORITE ACTIVITIES WERE . . .

1.

2.

3

MY TRIP WAS

/10

JAN   FEB   MAR   APR   MAY   JUN   JUL   AUG   SEP   OCT   NOV   DEC
1 2 3 4 5 6 7 8 9 10 11 12 13 14 15 16 17 18 19 20 21 22 23 24 25 26 27 28 29 30 31

CARLSBAD CAVERNS

NEW MEXICO

VISITORS CENTER: Carlsbad Caverns National Park Visitor Center

WHEN TO GO: The temperatures in the caves stay at 56°F throughout the year. In summer, hours are extended later in the afternoon.

LODGING: Backcountry camping (permit required)

HIKES:
Chihuahuan Desert Nature Trail I Carlsbad Caverns Desert Loop Road I Carlsbad Caverns Roadside Trail I Guadalupe Ridge Trail I Juniper Ridge Trail I Old Guano Trail I Walnut Canyon Overlook Trail I Yucca Canyon Trail

CAVE TOURS:
Easy: Big Room Trail (self-guided) I King's Palace Tour
Moderate: Slaughter Canyon Cave Tour
Strenuous: Hall of the White Giant Tour I Left Hand Tunnel Tour I Lower Cave Tour I Natural Entrance Trail (self-guided)

ACTIVITIES:
Bat Flight Program I Bird-watching at the official Audubon Important Bird Area I Black River Recreation Area I McDonald Observatory I Picnicking at Rattlesnake Springs

WILDLIFE SPOTTING:
Bell's vireos I Blanchard's cricket frogs I Brazilian free-tailed bats I Cave swallows I Eastern barking frogs I Eastern bluebirds I Hooded orioles I Plain-bellied water snakes I Summer tanagers I Wild turkeys I Yellow-billed cuckoos

DATE VISITED:

WEATHER:

WHERE I WENT:

WHERE I STAYED:

WHO I WENT WITH:

FAVORITE MOMENT:

WHAT I'D RECOMMEND:

TIPS TO FRIENDS/ FAMILY:

WHAT I WISH I KNEW BEFORE GOING:

WHAT WAS THE FIRST THING I NOTICED WHEN I ARRIVED?

MY FAVORITE PART OF THE VISIT WAS . . .

HOW I SPENT MY TIME THERE:

WHAT WOULD I DO IF I GO BACK?

WHAT IS SOMETHING NEW I LEARNED?

MY TOP THREE FAVORITE ACTIVITIES WERE . . .

1.

2.

3

MY TRIP WAS

/10

JAN   FEB   MAR   APR   MAY   JUN   JUL   AUG   SEP   OCT   NOV   DEC
1 2 3 4 5 6 7 8 9 10 11 12 13 14 15 16 17 18 19 20 21 22 23 24 25 26 27 28 29 30 31

GUADALUPE MOUNTAINS

TEXAS

 VISITORS CENTERS: Dog Canyon Ranger Station I McKittrick Canyon Visitor Center I Pine Springs Visitor Center

 WHEN TO GO: Fall is the best time for hiking, but it is often crowded, whereas May and June are very hot in the lowlands; late summer rains offer some respite.

LODGING: Three campgrounds (tents, RVs, horses)

● **HIKES:**
Easy: Foothills Trail I Guadalupe Salt Basin Dunes I Manzanita Spring Trail I McKittrick Canyon Nature Trail I Pinery Trail I Smith Spring Trail
Moderate: El Capitan Trail I Foothills Loop I Lost Peak via Tejas Trail I Marcus Overlook via Bush Mountain Trail I McKittrick Canyon Trail I Pratt Cabin via McKittrick Canyon Trail
Difficult: Bowl Loop Trail I Devil's Hall Trail I Guadalupe Peak Trail I Hunter Peak I Permian Reef Trail I The Notch Hike

● **ACTIVITIES:**
Driving through Dog Canyon I El Capitan Viewpoint I Guadalupe Peak Viewpoint I Horseback riding I Salt Basin Dunes I Seeing changing fall colors

● **WILDLIFE SPOTTING:**
Black bears I Black-tailed jackrabbits I Broad-tailed hummingbirds I Elk I Gray foxes I Mountain chickadees I Mountain lions I Mountain short-horned lizards I Mule deer I Porcupines I Say's phoebes I Skunks I Steller's jays

---

DATE VISITED:

WEATHER:

WHERE I WENT:

WHERE I STAYED:

WHO I WENT WITH:

FAVORITE MOMENT:

WHAT I'D RECOMMEND:

TIPS TO FRIENDS/ FAMILY:

WHAT I WISH I KNEW BEFORE GOING:

WHAT WAS THE FIRST THING I NOTICED WHEN I ARRIVED?

MY FAVORITE PART
OF THE VISIT WAS . . .

HOW I SPENT MY TIME THERE:

WHAT WOULD I DO IF I GO BACK?

WHAT IS SOMETHING
NEW I LEARNED?

MY TOP THREE FAVORITE ACTIVITIES WERE . . .

1.

2.

3

MY TRIP
WAS

/10

JAN   FEB   MAR   APR   MAY   JUN   JUL   AUG   SEP   OCT   NOV   DEC
1 2 3 4 5 6 7 8 9 10 11 12 13 14 15 16 17 18 19 20 21 22 23 24 25 26 27 28 29 30 31

HOT SPRINGS

ARKANSAS

 VISITORS CENTER: Fordyce Bathhouse Visitor Center

WHEN TO GO: You can enjoy the park year-round, but late spring and fall are the most pleasant seasons; summers can be hot and crowded.

LODGING: One camp-ground (tents, RVs) I Hotel Hale

● **HIKES:**

Easy: Honeysuckle Trail I Hot Springs Mountain Trail I Lower Dogwood Trail I Peak Trail I Upper Dogwood Trail I West Mountain Trail
Moderate: Goat Rock Trail I Gulpha Gorge Trail I Oertel Trail
Difficult: Sunset Trail

● **ACTIVITIES:**

Bathhouse Row I Buckstaff Bathhouse I Fordyce Bathhouse Museum I Grand Promenade I Quapaw Baths and Spa I Superior Bathhouse Brewery I West Mountain Scenic Drive

● **WILDLIFE SPOTTING:**

Banded darters I Black bears I Bluegills I Cedar waxwings I Chipmunks I Frogs I Grass carp I Groundhogs I Spotted sala-manders I Squirrels I White-tailed deer

---

DATE VISITED:

WEATHER:

WHERE I WENT:

WHERE I STAYED:

WHO I WENT WITH:

FAVORITE MOMENT:

WHAT I'D RECOMMEND:

TIPS TO FRIENDS/ FAMILY:

WHAT I WISH I KNEW BEFORE GOING:

WHAT WAS THE FIRST THING I NOTICED WHEN I ARRIVED?

MY FAVORITE PART OF THE VISIT WAS . . .

HOW I SPENT MY TIME THERE:

WHAT WOULD I DO IF I GO BACK?

WHAT IS SOMETHING NEW I LEARNED?

MY TOP THREE FAVORITE ACTIVITIES WERE . . .

1.

2.

3

MY TRIP WAS

/10

WHITE SANDS
NEW MEXICO

VISITORS CENTER: White Sands Visitor Center

WHEN TO GO: Fall is usually the most pleasant time to visit the park. Summers can be very hot, topping 100°F. Thunderstorms are common from July to September.

LODGING: No camping or lodging inside the park

- **HIKES:**
Easy: Dune Life Nature Trail I Interdune Boardwalk I Lake Lucero Path I Playa Trail
Moderate: Alkali Flat Trail I White Sands Backcountry Trail

- **ACTIVITIES:**
Bicycling I Dunes Drive I Full moon hike (ranger-led) I Full moon night gazing I Visiting the native plant garden I Roadrunner Picnic Area I Sand sledding I Sunset Stroll (ranger-led)

- **WILDLIFE SPOTTING:**
American badgers I Barn swallows I Black-chinned hummingbirds I Bleached earless lizards I Bobcats I Burrowing owls I Cactus wrens I Coyotes I Foxes I Pallid bats I Pocket gophers I Roadrunners

---

DATE VISITED:

WEATHER:

WHERE I WENT:

WHERE I STAYED:

WHO I WENT WITH:

FAVORITE MOMENT:

WHAT I'D RECOMMEND:

TIPS TO FRIENDS/FAMILY:

WHAT I WISH I KNEW BEFORE GOING:

WHAT WAS THE FIRST THING I NOTICED WHEN I ARRIVED?

MY FAVORITE PART
OF THE VISIT WAS . . .

HOW I SPENT MY TIME THERE:

WHAT WOULD I DO IF I GO BACK?

WHAT IS SOMETHING
NEW I LEARNED?

MY TOP THREE FAVORITE ACTIVITIES WERE . . .

1.

2.

3

MY TRIP
WAS

/10

ARCHES

UTAH

ARCHES
EST 1971

VISITORS CENTER: Arches National Park Visitor Center

WHEN TO GO: Spring storms bring April and May wildflowers, while monsoons can come through in July and August causing wildflower blooms in early fall. Snowfall can be seen November through February.

LODGING: Backcountry camping (permit required) I One campground (tents)

HIKES:

Easy: Arches Visitor Center Nature Trail I Balanced Rock Trail I Broken Arch Trail I Double Arch Trail I Landscape Arch Trail I Navajo Arch Trail I Park Avenue Trail I Partition Arch Trail I Pine Tree Arch Trail I Sand Dune Arch Trail I Skyline Arch Trail I Tunnel Arch Trail I Windows Loop Trail
Moderate: Delicate Arch Trail I Double O Arch Trail I Eye of the Whale Trail I Lower Courthouse Wash Trail I Tower Arch Trail
Difficult: Devils Garden Trail I Elephant Butte

ACTIVITIES:

Arches Scenic Drive I Canyoneering I Ranger-guided tours I Road biking I Rock climbing I Stargazing

WILDLIFE SPOTTING:

Antelope squirrels I Black-tailed jackrabbits I Chipmunks I Coyotes I Desert cottontails I Eagles I Hawks I Kangaroo rats I Mule deer I Porcupines I Rock squirrels I Skunks

---

DATE VISITED:

WEATHER:

WHERE I WENT:

WHERE I STAYED:

WHO I WENT WITH:

FAVORITE MOMENT:

WHAT I'D RECOMMEND:

TIPS TO FRIENDS/ FAMILY:

WHAT I WISH I KNEW BEFORE GOING:

WHAT WAS THE FIRST THING I NOTICED WHEN I ARRIVED?

MY FAVORITE PART OF THE VISIT WAS . . .

HOW I SPENT MY TIME THERE:

WHAT WOULD I DO IF I GO BACK?

WHAT IS SOMETHING NEW I LEARNED?

MY TOP THREE FAVORITE ACTIVITIES WERE . . .

1.

2.

3

MY TRIP WAS

/10

JAN   FEB   MAR   APR   MAY   JUN   JUL   AUG   SEP   OCT   NOV   DEC
1 2 3 4 5 6 7 8 9 10 11 12 13 14 15 16 17 18 19 20 21 22 23 24 25 26 27 28 29 30 31

BLACK CANYON OF THE GUNNISON

COLORADO

VISITORS CENTERS: South Rim Visitor Center I North Rim Ranger Station

WHEN TO GO: Wildflowers peak in June, and hiking is superb in early fall. But thunderstorms add afternoon drama in July and August.

LODGING: Three campgrounds (tents, RVs)

- **HIKES:**

Easy: Cedar Point Nature Trail I Dragon Point Trail I Gunnison Point Overlook I Painted Wall View Trail I Uplands Trail I Warner Point Nature Trail

Moderate: Chasm View Nature Trail I Deadhorse Loop Trail I North Vista Trail to Exclamation Point I Rim Rock Nature Trail I Oak Flat Loop Trail

Difficult: Gunnison Route Trail (permit required) I Tomichi Trail I Warner Route

- **ACTIVITIES:**

Driving the South Rim I Driving the North Rim I Kayaking/rafting the Gunnison River I Gunnison Tunnel I Rock climbing I Stargazing I Trout fishing

- **WILDLIFE SPOTTING:**

Bald eagles I Bighorn sheep I Black bears I Brown trout I Cutthroat trout I Elk I Golden eagles I Mule deer I Otters I Peregrine falcons I Rainbow trout I Yellow-bellied marmots

---

DATE VISITED:

WEATHER:

WHERE I WENT:

WHERE I STAYED:

WHO I WENT WITH:

FAVORITE MOMENT:

WHAT I'D RECOMMEND:

TIPS TO FRIENDS/ FAMILY:

WHAT I WISH I KNEW BEFORE GOING:

WHAT WAS THE FIRST THING I NOTICED WHEN I ARRIVED?

MY FAVORITE PART OF THE VISIT WAS . . .

HOW I SPENT MY TIME THERE:

WHAT WOULD I DO IF I GO BACK?

WHAT IS SOMETHING NEW I LEARNED?

MY TOP THREE FAVORITE ACTIVITIES WERE . . .

1.

2.

3

MY TRIP WAS

/10

BRYCE CANYON

UTAH

VISITORS CENTER: Bryce Canyon National Park Visitor Center

WHEN TO GO: Fall and spring bring cooler temperatures as well as beautiful foliage and wildflowers. Summer temperatures get up to 80°F and mean large crowds. Winter is great for scenic drives or snowshoe hikes.

LODGING: Backcountry camping (permit required) I Two campgrounds (tents, RVs) I The Lodge at Bryce Canyon

HIKES:
Easy: Bristlecone Loop Trail I Bryce Point Trail I Mossy Cave Trail I Piracy Point I Sunset Point to Sunrise Point I Upper Inspiration Point Trail I Yovimpa Point
Moderate: Bryce Canyon Rim Trail I Navajo Loop Trail I Queens Garden Trail I Swamp Canyon Trail I Tower Bridge Trail
Difficult: Fairyland Loop I Hat Shop Trail I Peek-A-Boo Loop I Riggs Spring Loop Trail I Under-the-Rim Trail

ACTIVITIES:
Bike riding on shared-use path I Bryce Canyon Southern Scenic Drive I Horseback riding tours I Ranger-led moonlit hikes I Snowshoe tours I Bryce Amphitheater I Telescope stargazing

WILDLIFE SPOTTING:
Black-chinned hummingbirds I Bobcats I Chickadees I Coyotes I Finches I Flycatchers I Green-tailed towhees I Mule deer I Nuthatches I Peregrine falcons I Porcupines I Prairie dogs I Pronghorn I Steller's jays I Swallows I Uinta chipmunks I Western wood-pewees I Yellow-rumped warblers

DATE VISITED:

WEATHER:

WHERE I WENT:

WHERE I STAYED:

WHO I WENT WITH:

FAVORITE MOMENT:

WHAT I'D RECOMMEND:

TIPS TO FRIENDS/ FAMILY:

WHAT I WISH I KNEW BEFORE GOING:

WHAT WAS THE FIRST THING I NOTICED WHEN I ARRIVED?

MY FAVORITE PART OF THE VISIT WAS . . .

HOW I SPENT MY TIME THERE:

WHAT WOULD I DO IF I GO BACK?

WHAT IS SOMETHING NEW I LEARNED?

MY TOP THREE FAVORITE ACTIVITIES WERE . . .

1.

2.

3

MY TRIP WAS

/10

JAN   FEB   MAR   APR   MAY   JUN   JUL   AUG   SEP   OCT   NOV   DEC
1 2 3 4 5 6 7 8 9 10 11 12 13 14 15 16 17 18 19 20 21 22 23 24 25 26 27 28 29 30 31

CANYONLANDS
UTAH

VISITORS CENTERS: Canyonlands Backcountry Office I Hans Flat (Maze) Ranger Station I Island in the Sky Visitor Center I The Needles Visitor Center

WHEN TO GO: Spring and fall are ideal for hiking, though weather is temperamental. Summer temperatures can bring triple digits and monsoons. Even mild winters can shut down roads.

LODGING: Backcountry camping (permit required) I Three campgrounds (tents, RVs)

HIKES:

Easy: Elephant Hill Trail I Grand View Point Trail I Green River Overlook I Mesa Arch Trail I Murphy Point Trail I Pothole Point Trail I Whale Rock Trail I White Rim Overlook Trail

Moderate: Aztec Butte Trail I Big Spring Canyon Overlook I Cave Spring Trail I Chesler Park Loop Trail I Confluence Overlook Trail I Devil's Pocket Loop I Druid Arch Trail I Flint Trail I Horseshoe Canyon Trail I Maze Overlook Trail I Neck Spring Trail I Shafer Trail I Slickrock Trail I Upheaval Dome via Crater View Trail

Difficult: Gooseberry Trail I Lower Red Lake Canyon Trail I Syncline Loop

ACTIVITIES:

Dead Horse Point State Park I Glen Canyon National Recreation Area I Scott and Norma Matheson Wetlands Preserve I Manti-La Sal National Forest I Sand Flats Recreation Area I Westwater Canyon Wilderness Study Area I White Rim Road Drive

WILDLIFE SPOTTING:

Antelope squirrels I Black-tailed jackrabbits I Chipmunks I Coyotes I Desert cottontails I Kangaroo rats I Mule deer I Muskrats I Northern leopard frogs I Porcupines I Skunks I Wood rats

---

DATE VISITED:

WEATHER:

WHERE I WENT:

WHERE I STAYED:

WHO I WENT WITH:

FAVORITE MOMENT:

WHAT I'D RECOMMEND:

TIPS TO FRIENDS/ FAMILY:

WHAT I WISH I KNEW BEFORE GOING:

WHAT WAS THE FIRST THING I NOTICED WHEN I ARRIVED?

MY FAVORITE PART OF THE VISIT WAS . . .

HOW I SPENT MY TIME THERE:

WHAT WOULD I DO IF I GO BACK?

WHAT IS SOMETHING NEW I LEARNED?

MY TOP THREE FAVORITE ACTIVITIES WERE . . .

1.

2.

3

MY TRIP WAS

/10

CAPITOL REEF

UTAH

VISITORS CENTER: Capitol Reef Visitor Center

WHEN TO GO: Spring brings orchard blossoms and ideal hiking temperatures; summer temperatures hover in the 90s but are cool in the evening. Fall ushers in cooler temperatures, and intermittent snow cover makes winter a wonderland.

LODGING: Backcountry camping (permit required) I Three campgrounds (tents, RVs)

HIKES:
Easy: Cathedrals Trail I Gooseneck Overlook Trail I Grand Wash Trail I Morrell Cabin Trail I Panorama Point I Petroglyph Trail I Pioneer Register Trail I Red Canyon Trail I Sulphur Creek Waterfall Hike I Sunset Point Trail
Moderate: Burro Wash Trail I Capitol Gorge Trail I Cassidy Arch Trail I Chimney Rock Loop Trail I Cohab Canyon Trail I Cottonwood Wash I Fremont River Trail I Fruita Trail I Frying Pan Trail I Golden Throne Trail I Hickman Bridge Trail I Lower Spring Canyon Trail I Pleasant Creek Trail I Sulphur Creek Route I Surprise Canyon Route I Upper Muley Twist
Difficult: Brimhall Natural Bridge I Navajo Knobs Trail I Old Wagon Loop Trail I Sheets Gulch Trail I Lower Muley Twist Canyon

ACTIVITIES:
Four-wheel driving through Cathedral Valley I Capitol Reef Scenic Drive I Fruita Historic District I Fruita Schoolhouse I Gifford Homestead I Notom-Bullfrog Road I Utah Scenic Byway 24 drive

WILDLIFE SPOTTING:
American beavers I Bighorn sheep I Bullock's orioles I Canyon bats I Fairy shrimp I Golden eagles I Gray foxes I Mexican spotted owls I Mountain bluebirds I Mountain lions I Mule deer I Peregrine falcons I Ringtails I Rock squirrels I Water striders I White-tailed antelope squirrels I Yellow-bellied marmots

---

DATE VISITED:

WEATHER:

WHERE I WENT:

WHERE I STAYED:

WHO I WENT WITH:

FAVORITE MOMENT:

WHAT I'D RECOMMEND:

TIPS TO FRIENDS/ FAMILY:

WHAT I WISH I KNEW BEFORE GOING:

WHAT WAS THE FIRST THING I NOTICED WHEN I ARRIVED?

MY FAVORITE PART OF THE VISIT WAS . . .

HOW I SPENT MY TIME THERE:

WHAT WOULD I DO IF I GO BACK?

WHAT IS SOMETHING NEW I LEARNED?

MY TOP THREE FAVORITE ACTIVITIES WERE . . .

1.

2.

3

MY TRIP WAS

/10

JAN   FEB   MAR   APR   MAY   JUN   JUL   AUG   SEP   OCT   NOV   DEC
1 2 3 4 5 6 7 8 9 10 11 12 13 14 15 16 17 18 19 20 21 22 23 24 25 26 27 28 29 30 31

....

....

....

....

....

....

....

....

....

....

....

....

....

....

....

....

....

....

....

....

....

....

....

GRAND CANYON

ARIZONA

VISITORS CENTERS: Grand Canyon Visitor Center (South Rim) | North Rim Visitor Center | Verkamp's Visitor Center

WHEN TO GO: Summer and school vacation times are peak season, so visit from November to March to avoid crowds.

LODGING: Five campgrounds (tents) | Bright Angel Lodge | El Tovar Hotel | Kachina Lodge | Maswik Lodge | Phantom Ranch | Thunderbird Lodge | Yavapai Lodge

---

HIKES:

Easy: Bright Angel Point Trail | Cape Final Trail | Cape Royal Trail | Cliff Spring Trail | Coconino Overlook | Desert View Watchtower via Visitor Center Trail | Grand Canyon Bridle Trail | Grand Canyon Greenway Trail | Grand Canyon Rim Trail | Mather Point | Point Imperial | Roosevelt Point Trail | Shoshone Point | Trail of Time | Uncle Jim Trail
Moderate: Havasu Canyon Trail | Hopi Point | Mohave Point | Supai Tunnel | Transept Trail | Widforss Trail
Difficult: Bright Angel Trail | Grandview Trail | Hermit Trail | New Hance Trail | North Kaibab Trail | South Kaibab Trail | Tanner Trail | Tonto Trail

ACTIVITIES:

Boating/kayaking/white-water rafting the Colorado River | Desert View | Desert View Scenic Drive | Hermit Road Shuttle | Historic Village | Hopi House | Kolb Studio | Lookout Studio | Phantom Ranch stay (accessible only by foot, mule, or boat) | Yavapai Point Museum

WILDLIFE SPOTTING:

Bald eagles | Bats | Beavers | Bighorn sheep | California condors | Coyotes | Desert spiny lizards | Desert tortoises | Falcons | Grand Canyon elk | Gray foxes | Great horned owls | Mountain lions | Mule deer | Peregrine falcons | Pygmy owls

---

DATE VISITED:

WEATHER:

WHERE I WENT:

WHERE I STAYED:

WHO I WENT WITH:

FAVORITE MOMENT:

WHAT I'D RECOMMEND:

TIPS TO FRIENDS/ FAMILY:

WHAT I WISH I KNEW BEFORE GOING:

WHAT WAS THE FIRST THING I NOTICED WHEN I ARRIVED?

MY FAVORITE PART OF THE VISIT WAS . . .

HOW I SPENT MY TIME THERE:

WHAT WOULD I DO IF I GO BACK?

WHAT IS SOMETHING NEW I LEARNED?

MY TOP THREE FAVORITE ACTIVITIES WERE . . .

1.

2.

3

MY TRIP WAS

/10

JAN   FEB   MAR   APR   MAY   JUN   JUL   AUG   SEP   OCT   NOV   DEC
1 2 3 4 5 6 7 8 9 10 11 12 13 14 15 16 17 18 19 20 21 22 23 24 25 26 27 28 29 30 31

GREAT BASIN

NEVADA

 **VISITORS CENTERS:** Great Basin National Park Visitor Center I Lehman Caves Visitor Center

WHEN TO GO: Spring and fall are best for hiking, while summer has the highest number of visitors. Wheeler Peak Scenic Drive generally closes November to May.

LODGING: Six campgrounds (tents, RVs)

- **HIKES:**
Easy: Alpine Lakes Loop Trail I Sky Islands Forest Trail I Lehman Cave I Osceola Ditch Interpretive Trail
Moderate: Bristlecone Pine Glacier Trail I Lexington Arch Trail I Pole Canyon Trail I Serviceberry Loop I Snake Creek Overlook I South Fork Baker Creek Trail I Stella Lake Trail I Strawberry Creek Trail I Teresa Lake
Difficult: Baker Creek Loop I Baker Lake Trail I Baker Lake-Johnson Lake Loop I Dead Lake Trail I Lehman Creek Trail I Timber Creek Loop I Wheeler Peak Trail

- **ACTIVITIES:**
Baker Village Archaeological Site I Lehman Caves Tours (Grand Palace and Lodge Room) I Wheeler Peak Scenic Drive I Upper Pictograph Cave

- **WILDLIFE SPOTTING:**
Badgers I Beavers I Big brown bats I Bighorn sheep I Bobcats I Cutthroat trout I Golden eagles I Killdeer I Porcupines I Pygmy rabbits I Ringtails I Sagebrush voles I Water shrews I Yellow-bellied marmots

DATE VISITED:

WEATHER:

WHERE I WENT:

WHERE I STAYED:

WHO I WENT WITH:

FAVORITE MOMENT:

WHAT I'D RECOMMEND:

TIPS TO FRIENDS/ FAMILY:

WHAT I WISH I KNEW BEFORE GOING:

WHAT WAS THE FIRST THING I NOTICED WHEN I ARRIVED?

MY FAVORITE PART OF THE VISIT WAS . . .

HOW I SPENT MY TIME THERE:

WHAT WOULD I DO IF I GO BACK?

WHAT IS SOMETHING NEW I LEARNED?

MY TOP THREE FAVORITE ACTIVITIES WERE . . .

1.

2.

3

MY TRIP WAS

/10

JAN   FEB   MAR   APR   MAY   JUN   JUL   AUG   SEP   OCT   NOV   DEC

1 2 3 4 5 6 7 8 9 10 11 12 13 14 15 16 17 18 19 20 21 22 23 24 25 26 27 28 29 30 31

MESA VERDE

COLORADO

 **VISITORS CENTER:** Mesa Verde Visitor and Research Center

WHEN TO GO: The park is open year-round, but many roads, including Cliff Palace Loop, and archaeological sites are closed during the winter.

LODGING: One campground (tents, RVs) I Far View Lodge

● **HIKES:**

Easy: Badger House Community Trail I Balcony House Loop Trail I Cliff Palace Loop Trail I Far View Sites Complex I Farming Terrace Trail I Knife Edge Trail I Nordenskiöld Site No. 16 Trail I Park Point Overlook Trail I Soda Canyon Overlook Trail I Square Tower House Overlook I Tower Overlook Trail

Moderate: Long House Trail I Mesa Verde Point Lookout Trail I Petroglyph Point Trail I Prater Ridge Trail I Spruce Canyon Trail I Step House Trail I Wetherill Mesa Loop

● **ACTIVITIES:**

Bird-watching I Cliff dwelling tours I Four Corners Lecture Series I Geologic Overlook I Ranger-led tours I Mesa Top Loop Road I Mesa Verde National Park Scenic Drive I Wetherill Mesa

● **WILDLIFE SPOTTING:**

Black bears I Black-chinned hummingbirds I Bobcats I Collared lizards I Cottontails I Coyotes I Elk I Great horned owls I Mountain short-horned lizards I Mule deer I Prairie rattlesnakes I Spotted bats I Spotted owls I Weasels I Wild turkeys I Woodhouse's toads

---

DATE VISITED:

WEATHER:

WHERE I WENT:

WHERE I STAYED:

WHO I WENT WITH:

FAVORITE MOMENT:

WHAT I'D RECOMMEND:

TIPS TO FRIENDS/ FAMILY:

WHAT I WISH I KNEW BEFORE GOING:

WHAT WAS THE FIRST THING I NOTICED WHEN I ARRIVED?

MY FAVORITE PART
OF THE VISIT WAS . . .

HOW I SPENT MY TIME THERE:

WHAT WOULD I DO IF I GO BACK?

WHAT IS SOMETHING
NEW I LEARNED?

MY TOP THREE FAVORITE ACTIVITIES WERE . . .

1.

2.

3

MY TRIP
WAS

/10

PETRIFIED FOREST

ARIZONA

VISITORS CENTERS: Painted Desert Visitor Center I Rainbow Forest Museum

WHEN TO GO: Summer is the most popular season, but temperatures can get hot. Fall and even winter are more temperate, and spring is the best for blooming wildflowers.

LODGING: Backcountry camping (permit required)

HIKES:
Easy: Agate House Trail I Billings Gap Overlook I Blue Mesa Trail I Crystal Forest Trail I Giant Logs Trail I Long Logs Trail I Old Jasper Forest Road I Painted Desert Rim Trail I Puerco Pueblo Trail I Tawa Trail
Moderate: Devil's Playground Loop I First Forest Point I Historic Blue Forest Trail I Onyx Bridge Trail

ACTIVITIES:
Biking the Tepees I Geocaching I Museum Demonstration Lab I Newspaper Rock I Painted Desert Inn National Historic Landmark I Painted Desert Overlooks I Petrified Forest Scenic Drive I Puerco Pueblo I Rainbow Forest Museum I Ranger-led tours

WILDLIFE SPOTTING:
American avocets I Badgers I Barn owls I Bobcats I Cottontail rabbits I Coyotes I Deer mice I Desert shrews I Gophers I Mexican wood rats I Mule deer I New Mexico whiptails I Pallid bats I Pronghorn I Striped skunks

DATE VISITED:

WEATHER:

WHERE I WENT:

WHERE I STAYED:

WHO I WENT WITH:

FAVORITE MOMENT:

WHAT I'D RECOMMEND:

TIPS TO FRIENDS/ FAMILY:

WHAT I WISH I KNEW BEFORE GOING:

WHAT WAS THE FIRST THING I NOTICED WHEN I ARRIVED?

MY FAVORITE PART OF THE VISIT WAS . . .

HOW I SPENT MY TIME THERE:

WHAT WOULD I DO IF I GO BACK?

WHAT IS SOMETHING NEW I LEARNED?

MY TOP THREE FAVORITE ACTIVITIES WERE . . .

1.

2.

3

MY TRIP WAS

/10

SAGUARO

ARIZONA

 **VISITORS CENTERS:** Red Hills Visitor Center I Rincon Mountain Visitor Center

 **WHEN TO GO:** October through April temperatures are the most pleasant, while summer is very hot and thunderstorms can cause flash floods.

 **LODGING:** Backcountry camping in the Rincon Mountain District only (permit required)

- **HIKES:**

Easy: Cactus Garden Trail I Desert Discovery Nature Trail I Desert Ecology Trail I Freeman Homestead Nature Trail I Garwood Trail I Loma Verde and Squeeze Pen Loop I Mica View Trail I Signal Hill Trail I Valley View Overlook Trail
Moderate: Bridal Wreath Falls Trail I Cactus Forest Trail I Cactus Wren Trail I Douglas Spring Trail I Ernie's Falls I Gould Mine Trail I Hope Camp Trail I Hugh Norris Trail I Ridge View Trail I Sendero Esperanza Trail I Thunderbird Trail I Wildhorse Trail
Difficult: Manning Camp Trail I Rincon Peak Trail I Tanque Verde Peak I Turkey Creek I Wasson Peak

- **ACTIVITIES:**

Arizona-Sonora Desert Museum I Bajada Loop Drive I Biking I Cactus Forest I Guided ranger programs I Petroglyphs at Signal Hill I Scenic Loop Drive I Sunset viewing

- **WILDLIFE SPOTTING:**

Antelope jackrabbits I Bobcats I Coyotes I Gambel's quails I Gila woodpeckers I Gray foxes I Ground squirrels I Javelinas I Mountain lions I Mule deer I Pack rats I Ringtails I White-nosed coatis I White-tailed deer

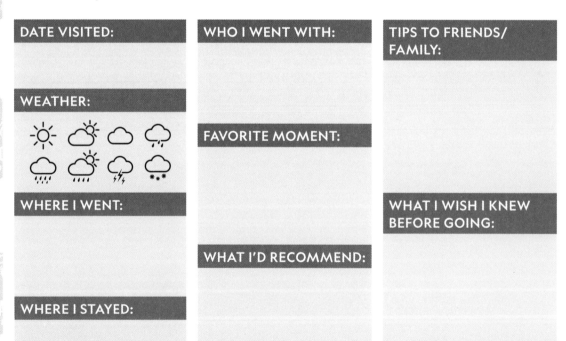

DATE VISITED:

WEATHER:

WHERE I WENT:

WHERE I STAYED:

WHO I WENT WITH:

FAVORITE MOMENT:

WHAT I'D RECOMMEND:

TIPS TO FRIENDS/ FAMILY:

WHAT I WISH I KNEW BEFORE GOING:

WHAT WAS THE FIRST THING I NOTICED WHEN I ARRIVED?

MY FAVORITE PART
OF THE VISIT WAS . . .

HOW I SPENT MY TIME THERE:

WHAT WOULD I DO IF I GO BACK?

WHAT IS SOMETHING
NEW I LEARNED?

MY TOP THREE FAVORITE ACTIVITIES WERE . . .

1.

2.

3

MY TRIP
WAS

/10

ZION

UTAH

VISITORS CENTERS: Kolob Canyons Visitor Center I Zion National Park Visitor Center I Zion Human History Museum

WHEN TO GO: The park is busy throughout the year. Spring and fall are the most rewarding in terms of weather and active wildlife, whereas summer can reach above 100°F and flash floods can occur.

LODGING: Backcountry camping (permit required) I Three campgrounds (tents, RVs) I Zion Lodge

---

HIKES:

Easy: Archeology Trail I Clear Creek Wash I Court of the Patriarchs Viewpoint Trail I Lava Point Overlook I Pa'rus Trail I Timber Creek Overlook Trail I Virgin River Walk I Weeping Rock Trail I Zion Grotto Trail I Zion Narrows Riverside Walk

Moderate: Chinle Trail I Coalpits Wash Trail I Emerald Pools Trail I Grapevine Trail I Kayenta Trail I Lower Pine Creek Waterfall Trail I Many Pools Trail I Sand Bench Trail I North Fork Taylor Creek I Two Pine Arch Trail I Watchman Trail I Wildcat Canyon Trail I Zion Canyon Overlook Trail

Difficult: Angels Landing Trail I Checkerboard Mesa Canyon Trail I East Temple Saddle Trail I La Verkin Creek Trail I South Fork Taylor Creek Trail I The Subway Trail I Zion Narrows Bottom Up to Big Springs

ACTIVITIES:

Biking Zion Canyon I Kolob Canyons Scenic Drive I Zion Canyon Scenic Drive I Zion Human History Museum I Zion Lodge Castle Dome Café I Zion-Mount Carmel Tunnel

WILDLIFE SPOTTING:

Canyon tree frogs I Coyotes I Dragonflies I Flycatchers I Foxes I Hummingbirds I Kingfishers I Mexican spotted owls I Mule deer I Ringtails I Vireos I Warblers I Zion snails

---

DATE VISITED:

WEATHER:

WHERE I WENT:

WHERE I STAYED:

WHO I WENT WITH:

FAVORITE MOMENT:

WHAT I'D RECOMMEND:

TIPS TO FRIENDS/ FAMILY:

WHAT I WISH I KNEW BEFORE GOING:

WHAT WAS THE FIRST THING I NOTICED WHEN I ARRIVED?

MY FAVORITE PART
OF THE VISIT WAS . . .

HOW I SPENT MY TIME THERE:

WHAT WOULD I DO IF I GO BACK?

WHAT IS SOMETHING
NEW I LEARNED?

MY TOP THREE FAVORITE ACTIVITIES WERE . . .

1.

2.

3

MY TRIP
WAS

/10

GLACIER

MONTANA

VISITORS CENTERS: Apgar Visitor Center I St. Mary Visitor Center I Logan Pass Visitor Center

WHEN TO GO: June through September is the best time to visit because access to the park is reduced during early spring and late fall and many roads are closed in the winter.

LODGING: Ten campgrounds (tents, RVs) I Cedar Creek Lodge I Glacier Park Lodge I Granite Park Chalet I Lake McDonald Lodge I Many Glacier Hotel I Rising Sun Motor Inn & Cabins I Swiftcurrent Motor Inn & Cabins I Village Inn at Apgar

HIKES:
Easy: 1885 Trail I Hemlock Grove Boardwalk I Loop Brook Trail I Meeting of the Waters Loop I Redrock Falls via Swiftcurrent Pass I Rockgarden Trail I Swiftcurrent Nature Trail
Moderate: Avalanche Crest Trail I Balu Pass Trail I Bear Creek Falls I Beaver River Trail I Great Glacier Trail I Hidden Lake Overlook
Difficult: Abbott Ridge Trail I Asulkan Valley Trail I Avalanche Mountain Loop I The Garden Wall I Glacier Crest Trail I Granite Park Trail I Hermit Trail I Highline Trail I Perley Rock Trail I Rogers Pass and Sapphire Hut I Sir Donald Trail I Video Peak

ACTIVITIES:
Astronomy programs I Boat tours I Chief Mountain International Highway I Glacier Institute Field Courses I Going-to-the-Sun Road I Guided raft tours on Flathead River I Horseback riding I Native American speakers and special events I Ranger-led activities I Waterton Lakes National Park in Canada (passport required)

WILDLIFE SPOTTING:
Beavers I Bighorn sheep I Black bears I Bull trout I Eagles I Elk I Grizzly bears I Harlequin ducks I Lynx I Mountain goats I Pikas I Ptarmigans I Western painted turtles I Wolverines I Wolves

---

DATE VISITED:

WEATHER:

WHERE I WENT:

WHERE I STAYED:

WHO I WENT WITH:

FAVORITE MOMENT:

WHAT I'D RECOMMEND:

TIPS TO FRIENDS/ FAMILY:

WHAT I WISH I KNEW BEFORE GOING:

WHAT WAS THE FIRST THING I NOTICED WHEN I ARRIVED?

MY FAVORITE PART OF THE VISIT WAS . . .

HOW I SPENT MY TIME THERE:

WHAT WOULD I DO IF I GO BACK?

WHAT IS SOMETHING NEW I LEARNED?

MY TOP THREE FAVORITE ACTIVITIES WERE . . .

1.

2.

3

MY TRIP WAS

10

JAN   FEB   MAR   APR   MAY   JUN   JUL   AUG   SEP   OCT   NOV   DEC
1 2 3 4 5 6 7 8 9 10 11 12 13 14 15 16 17 18 19 20 21 22 23 24 25 26 27 28 29 30 31

GRAND TETON

WYOMING

VISITORS CENTERS: Craig Thomas Discovery & Visitor Center I Jenny Lake Ranger Station I Jenny Lake Visitor Center I Colter Bay Visitor Center I Laurance S. Rockefeller Preserve Center I Flagg Ranch Information Station I National Elk Refuge & Greater Yellowstone Visitor Center

WHEN TO GO: July and August, with wildflowers blooming and sporadic thunderstorms, have peak visitation. Winter is beautiful but challenging, with road closures.

LODGING: American Alpine Club Grand Teton Climbers' Ranch I Backcountry camping (permit required) I Seven campgrounds (tents, RVs) I Colter Bay Village (cabins) I Jackson Lake Lodge I Jenny Lake Lodge I Signal Mountain Lodge

HIKES:

Easy: Colter Bay Hermitage Point Trail I Colter Bay Lakeshore Trail I Colter Bay Village I Cunningham Cabin I Leigh Lake Trail I Moose Ponds Trail I Oxbow Bend Overlook I Schwabacher's Landing Trail I Taggart Lake Loop I Two Ocean Lake Trail
Moderate: Bradley Lake Trail I Cascade Canyon Trail I Grand View Point Trail I Hidden Falls via Jenny Lake Trail I Jenny Lake Trail I Phelps Lake Trail I Signal Mountain Trail I String Lake Trail I Teton Canyon Road
Difficult: Death Canyon to Static Peak Divide Junction I Holly Lake Trail I Lake Solitude Trail I Lake of the Crags Trail I Lupine Meadows Trail I Paintbrush Peak I Rendezvous Mountain Trail I Static Peak I Surprise and Amphitheater Lakes Trail I Teton Crest Trail

ACTIVITIES:

Paddling Colter Bay I Floating the Snake River I Fossil Butte National Monument I Gros Ventre Wilderness I Jackson National Fish Hatchery I John D. Rockefeller Jr. Memorial Parkway I Laurance S. Rockefeller Preserve I National Bighorn Sheep Center I National Elk Refuge I T. A. Moulton Barn

WILDLIFE SPOTTING:

Beavers I Bison I Black bears I Coyotes I Elk I Grizzly bears I Ground squirrels I Moose I Mule deer I Pikas I Pronghorn I Sage grouse I Sage thrashers I Yellow-bellied marmots

---

DATE VISITED:

WEATHER:

WHERE I WENT:

WHERE I STAYED:

WHO I WENT WITH:

FAVORITE MOMENT:

WHAT I'D RECOMMEND:

TIPS TO FRIENDS/ FAMILY:

WHAT I WISH I KNEW BEFORE GOING:

WHAT WAS THE FIRST THING I NOTICED WHEN I ARRIVED?

MY FAVORITE PART OF THE VISIT WAS . . .

HOW I SPENT MY TIME THERE:

WHAT WOULD I DO IF I GO BACK?

WHAT IS SOMETHING NEW I LEARNED?

MY TOP THREE FAVORITE ACTIVITIES WERE . . .

1.

2.

3

MY TRIP WAS

/10

GREAT SAND DUNES

COLORADO

 VISITORS CENTER: Great Sand Dunes Visitor Center

 WHEN TO GO: The park is open year-round. Spring weather ranges from sunny to snowy, while summer has warm days and cool nights, and fall brings peak color in the foliage.

LODGING: Backcountry camping (permit required) I One campground (tents, RVs)

HIKES:
Easy: Great Sand Dunes Viewpoint Trail I Montville Nature Trail I Sand Sheet Loop I Piñon Flats Campground Trail I Wellington Ditch Trail
Moderate: Dunes Overlook Trail I Medano Lake Trail I Mosca Pass Trail I Sand Dunes Loop I Sand Pit Trail I Sand Ramp Trail
Difficult: High Dune Trail I Star Dune Trail I Upper Sand Creek Lake Trail

ACTIVITIES:
Climbing, sandboarding, or sand sledding the dunefields I Medano Pass Primitive Road I Ranger-led programs/hikes I Wading in Medano Creek I Stargazing I Watching the sand-hill crane migration

WILDLIFE SPOTTING:
Abert's squirrels I Black bears I Green-tailed towhees I Ground squirrels I Kangaroo rats I Mice I Mountain bluebirds I Mule deer I Pronghorn I Western tanagers I White-tailed ptarmigans

---

DATE VISITED:

WEATHER:

WHERE I WENT:

WHERE I STAYED:

WHO I WENT WITH:

FAVORITE MOMENT:

WHAT I'D RECOMMEND:

TIPS TO FRIENDS/ FAMILY:

WHAT I WISH I KNEW BEFORE GOING:

WHAT WAS THE FIRST THING I NOTICED WHEN I ARRIVED?

MY FAVORITE PART OF THE VISIT WAS . . .

HOW I SPENT MY TIME THERE:

WHAT WOULD I DO IF I GO BACK?

WHAT IS SOMETHING NEW I LEARNED?

MY TOP THREE FAVORITE ACTIVITIES WERE . . .

1.

2.

3

MY TRIP WAS

JAN	FEB	MAR	APR	MAY	JUN	JUL	AUG	SEP	OCT	NOV	DEC
1 2 3	4 5 6	7 8 9	10 11	12	13 14	15 16 17	18 19 20	21 22	23 24	25 26 27	28 29 30 31

ROCKY MOUNTAIN

COLORADO

 VISITORS CENTERS: Alpine Visitor Center **I** Beaver Meadows Visitor Center **I** Fall River Visitor Center **I** Kawuneeche Visitor Center **I** Moraine Park Discovery Center **I** Sheep Lakes Information Station

WHEN TO GO: Summer and early fall are the most popular seasons. Although some roads might be closed from mid-October to Memorial Day, there are lots of activities to do in the winter.

LODGING: Backcountry camping (permit required) **I** Five campgrounds (tents, RVs)

HIKES:
Easy: Adams Falls Trail I Alberta Falls Trail I Alluvial Fan Trail I Alpine Ridge Trail I Bear Lake South Trails I Beaver Ponds I Dream Lake Trail I Emerald Lake Trail I Lily Lake Loop I Nymph Lake Trail I Sprague Lake Trail
Moderate: Cascade Falls I Cub Lake Loop Trail I Deer Mountain Trail I Fern Lake Trail I Four Lake Loop Trail I Gem Lake Trail I Lake Haiyaha I Timberline Falls via Glacier Gorge Loop
Difficult: Alberta Falls via Glacier Gorge and Fire Loop I Bluebird Lake Trail I Chasm Lake I Flattop Mountain Trail I Longs Peak Trail I Mount Lady Washington I Ouzel Lake Trail I Twin Sisters Peak Trail

ACTIVITIES:
Holzwarth Historic Site I Horseback riding I Old Fall River Road I Picnicking I Ranger-led programs I Sportfishing at Mills Lake I Trail Ridge Road I Wildlife-watching

WILDLIFE SPOTTING:
Beavers I Bighorn sheep I Black bears I Bobcats I Clark's nutcrackers I Coyotes I Eagles I Elk I Hawks I Moose I Mountain lions I Mule deer I Peregrine falcons I Pikas I Pine grosbeaks I Snowshoe hares I Western tanagers I Yellow-bellied marmots

DATE VISITED:

WEATHER:

WHERE I WENT:

WHERE I STAYED:

WHO I WENT WITH:

FAVORITE MOMENT:

WHAT I'D RECOMMEND:

TIPS TO FRIENDS/ FAMILY:

WHAT I WISH I KNEW BEFORE GOING:

WHAT WAS THE FIRST THING I NOTICED WHEN I ARRIVED?

MY FAVORITE PART OF THE VISIT WAS . . .

HOW I SPENT MY TIME THERE:

WHAT WOULD I DO IF I GO BACK?

WHAT IS SOMETHING NEW I LEARNED?

MY TOP THREE FAVORITE ACTIVITIES WERE . . .

1.

2.

3

MY TRIP WAS

/10

JAN   FEB   MAR   APR   MAY   JUN   JUL   AUG   SEP   OCT   NOV   DEC
1   2   3   4   5   6   7   8   9   10   11   12   13   14   15   16   17   18   19   20   21   22   23   24   25   26   27   28   29   30   31

YELLOWSTONE

WYOMING, IDAHO & MONTANA

 VISITORS CENTERS: Albright Visitor Center **I** Canyon Visitor Education Center **I** Fishing Bridge Visitor Center **I** Grant Visitor Center **I** Old Faithful Visitor Education Center **I** West Yellowstone Visitor Information Center

WHEN TO GO: Mid-June to Labor Day is high season, with spring coming in gradually and few visitors. Autumn brings warm days and cool nights. Yellowstone is open in the winter, but most roads and park facilities close October to mid-April.

LODGING: 10 campgrounds (tents, RVs) **I** Canyon Lodge and Cabins **I** Grant Village Lodge **I** Lake Yellowstone Hotel and Cabins **I** Old Faithful Inn **I** Roosevelt Lodge Cabins

HIKES:

Easy: Artist Point Trail **I** Biscuit Basin Interpretive Trail **I** Black Sand Basin Trail **I** Fairy Falls Trail **I** Grand Prismatic Springs **I** Lake Butte Overlook Trail **I** Lone Star Geyser Trail **I** Lost Lake Loop Trail **I** Midway Geyser Basin Trail **I** Moose Falls **I** Mystic Falls Trail **I** Norris Geyser Basin Trail **I** Old Faithful Geyser Loop Trail **I** Pelican Creek Nature Trail **I** Petrified Tree Trail **I** Wraith Falls Trail

Moderate: Beaver Ponds Loop Trail **I** Bunsen Peak Trail **I** Cascade Lake Trail **I** Purple Mountain Trail **I** Ribbon Lake Trail **I** Solitary Geyser **I** Natural Bridge Trail **I** Observation Point Trail

Difficult: Avalanche Peak Trail **I** Mount Washburn Trail **I** Osprey Falls Trail **I** Seven Mile Hole Trail **I** Slough Creek Trail

ACTIVITIES:

Canary Spring and Mammoth Hot Springs **I** Driving Dunraven Pass **I** Firehole Canyon Drive **I** Guided boat tour on Yellowstone Lake **I** Gull Point Drive **I** Lake Butte Scenic Drive **I** Mud Volcano **I** Museum of the National Park Ranger **I** Norris Geyser Basin Museum **I** Old Faithful Historic District

WILDLIFE SPOTTING:

Badgers **I** Bald eagles **I** Bison **I** Black-tailed deer **I** Bobcats **I** Cougars **I** Coyotes **I** Elk **I** Golden eagles **I** Gray wolves **I** Great gray owls **I** Great horned owls **I** Mule deer **I** Ospreys **I** Peregrine falcons **I** Pronghorn **I** River otters **I** Short-tailed weasels **I** Wolverines

DATE VISITED:

WEATHER:

WHERE I WENT:

WHERE I STAYED:

WHO I WENT WITH:

FAVORITE MOMENT:

WHAT I'D RECOMMEND:

TIPS TO FRIENDS/ FAMILY:

WHAT I WISH I KNEW BEFORE GOING:

WHAT WAS THE FIRST THING I NOTICED WHEN I ARRIVED?

MY FAVORITE PART OF THE VISIT WAS . . .

HOW I SPENT MY TIME THERE:

WHAT WOULD I DO IF I GO BACK?

WHAT IS SOMETHING NEW I LEARNED?

MY TOP THREE FAVORITE ACTIVITIES WERE . . .

1.

2.

3

MY TRIP WAS

JAN   FEB   MAR   APR   MAY   JUN   JUL   AUG   SEP   OCT   NOV   DEC
1 2 3 4 5 6 7 8 9 10 11 12 13 14 15 16 17 18 19 20 21 22 23 24 25 26 27 28 29 30 31

....

....

....

....

....

....

....

....

....

....

....

....

....

....

....

....

....

....

....

....

....

....

AMERICAN SAMOA

AMERICAN SAMOA

VISITORS CENTER: National Park of American Samoa Visitor Center

WHEN TO GO: Because American Samoa lies 14 degrees south of the Equator, the islands are always hot and humid, with the wet season occurring from October to May.

LODGING: Camping is prohibited I Vaoto Lodge on Ofu I Homestays on Ta'u I Colonial hotels on Tutuila

---

- **HIKES:**
Blunts Point I Ma Tree Walk I Oge Beach Trail I Si'u Point Trail I Tuafanua Trail

- **ACTIVITIES:**
Alofaaga Blowholes I Dave Barker's Eco Lodge I Dive Savaii I Downtown Pago Pago I Ecotours I EFKS Museum I Fagaloa Bay Scenic Drive I House of Rock I Lake Lanoto'o I Lovers Leap I Museum of Samoa I O Le Pupu-Pue National Park I Papase'ea Sliding Rocks I Paradise Beach I Pe'ape 'a Cave,

Upolu I Salamumu Beach I Saleaula Lava Field I Savaia Giant Clam Sanctuary I Snorkeling/kayaking with Samoa's 900 fish species I Tafua Crater I Tafua Peninsula Reserve I To Sua Ocean Trench I Vatia village

- **WILDLIFE SPOTTING:**
Anemonefish I Crimson-crowned fruit doves I Dolphins I Flying foxes I House geckos I Humpback whales I Orcas I Porpoises I Red parrotfish I Sea turtles I Tooth-billed pigeons

---

DATE VISITED:

WEATHER:

WHERE I WENT:

WHERE I STAYED:

WHO I WENT WITH:

FAVORITE MOMENT:

WHAT I'D RECOMMEND:

TIPS TO FRIENDS/ FAMILY:

WHAT I WISH I KNEW BEFORE GOING:

WHAT WAS THE FIRST THING I NOTICED WHEN I ARRIVED?

MY FAVORITE PART
OF THE VISIT WAS . . .

HOW I SPENT MY TIME THERE:

WHAT WOULD I DO IF I GO BACK?

WHAT IS SOMETHING
I LEARNED THERE?

MY TOP THREE FAVORITE ACTIVITIES WERE . . .

1.

2.

3

MY TRIP
WAS

/10

JAN   FEB   MAR   APR   MAY   JUN   JUL   AUG   SEP   OCT   NOV   DEC
1 2 3 4 5 6 7 8 9 10 11 12 13 14 15 16 17 18 19 20 21 22 23 24 25 26 27 28 29 30 31

CHANNEL ISLANDS

CALIFORNIA

 VISITORS CENTERS: Robert J. Lagomarsino Visitor Center I Outdoors Santa Barbara Visitor Center

WHEN TO GO: The park is open year-round. Summer offers ideal camping weather, while spring is the best for seeing wildflowers.

LODGING: Five campgrounds (tents) I Santa Cruz del Norte Backcountry (reservation required)

HIKES:

Easy: Becher's Bay Coastal Trail Hike I Cathedral Cove Hike I Cuyler Harbor Beach Hike I East Anacapa Island Trail I Historic Scorpion Ranch Hike I Inspiration Point Hike I Pinniped Point Hike I Prisoner's Harbor Hike I Water Canyon Beach Hike

Moderate: Arch Point Hike I Cavern Point Loop Hike I Cherry Canyon Hike I Del Norte Trail Overlook Hike I Potato Harbor Overlook Hike I Sea Lion Rookery I Water Canyon Hike

Difficult: Smuggler's Canyon Hike I Montañon Ridge Loop I San Pedro Point Hike I Chinese Harbor Hike I Pelican Bay Hike I Black Mountain Hike I Torrey Pines Hike I Skunk Point Hike I Carrington Point Hike I Lobo Canyon Hike I Cabrillo Monument Hike I Caliche Forest Hike I Point Bennett Hike I Cardwell Point Hike I Lester Point Hike I Crook Point Overlook Hike I Elephant Seal Cove Overlook Hike I Webster Point Hike I Signal Peak Hike

ACTIVITIES:
Anacapa Light Station I Bird-watching I Diving/snorkeling I Fishing I Kayaking I Painted Cave I Tide pooling I Vail & Vickers Ranch I Whale-watching

WILDLIFE SPOTTING:
Anacapa deer mice I Blue whales I California brown pelicans I California sea lions I Foxes I Gray whales I Great white sharks I Harbor seals I Humpback whales I Night lizards I Orcas I Salamanders I Scrub jays I Skunks I Western gulls

---

DATE VISITED:

WEATHER:

WHERE I WENT:

WHERE I STAYED:

WHO I WENT WITH:

FAVORITE MOMENT:

WHAT I'D RECOMMEND:

TIPS TO FRIENDS/ FAMILY:

WHAT I WISH I KNEW BEFORE GOING:

WHAT WAS THE FIRST THING I NOTICED WHEN I ARRIVED?

MY FAVORITE PART
OF THE VISIT WAS . . .

HOW I SPENT MY TIME THERE:

WHAT WOULD I DO IF I GO BACK?

WHAT IS SOMETHING
I LEARNED THERE?

MY TOP THREE FAVORITE ACTIVITIES WERE . . .

1.

2.

3

MY TRIP
WAS

/10

JAN   FEB   MAR   APR   MAY   JUN   JUL   AUG   SEP   OCT   NOV   DEC
1 2 3 4 5 6 7 8 9 10 11 12 13 14 15 16 17 18 19 20 21 22 23 24 25 26 27 28 29 30 31

DEATH VALLEY

CALIFORNIA & NEVADA

VISITORS CENTERS: Furnace Creek Visitor Center | Stovepipe Wells Ranger Station

WHEN TO GO: Late spring and late fall are the most pleasant seasons, but the park sees people year-round.

LODGING: Backcountry camping (permit required) | Seven campgrounds (tents, RVs) | Inn at Death Valley | Oasis at Death Valley | Panamint Springs Resort | Stovepipe Wells Village

---

HIKES:

Easy: Badwater Basin Salt Flats Trail | Dante's View Trail | Death Valley Natural Bridge Trail | Devils Golf Course Trail | Little Hebe Crater Trail | Mesquite Flat Sand Dunes Trail | Pride Rock Trail | Salt Creek Interpretive Trail | Texas Springs Trail | Zabriskie Point

Moderate: Coffin Peak | Desolation Canyon Trail | Golden Canyon Trail | Gower Gulch Loop Trail | Inyo Mine Trail | Mosaic Canyon Trail | Panamint Dunes Trail | Room Canyon Trail | Sidewinder Canyon Trail | Twenty Mule Team Canyon | Wildrose Peak Trail | Willow Canyon Trail

Difficult: Brown Peak | Corkscrew Peak | Cottonwood-Marble Canyon Loop (4WD required to reach this trail) | Funeral Canyon Hiking Route | Grotto Canyon | Indian Pass Trail | Little Bridge Canyon Trail | Kaleidoscope Canyon Trail | Keane Wonder Mine Trail | Mount Perry Trail | Telescope Peak Trail

ACTIVITIES:

Artist's Drive | Ashford Mill | Furnace Creek Ranch Golf Course | Harmony Borax Works | Mojave | Scotty's Castle | Ubehebe Crater | Wildrose Charcoal Kilns

WILDLIFE SPOTTING:

Bobcats | Desert bighorn sheep | Gophers | Jackrabbits | Kangaroo rats | Mojave Desert tortoises | Mountain lions | Roadrunners | Rufous hummingbirds | Squirrels

---

DATE VISITED:

WEATHER:

WHERE I WENT:

WHERE I STAYED:

WHO I WENT WITH:

FAVORITE MOMENT:

WHAT I'D RECOMMEND:

TIPS TO FRIENDS/FAMILY:

WHAT I WISH I KNEW BEFORE GOING:

WHAT WAS THE FIRST THING I NOTICED WHEN I ARRIVED?

MY FAVORITE PART OF THE VISIT WAS . . .

HOW I SPENT MY TIME THERE:

WHAT WOULD I DO IF I GO BACK?

WHAT IS SOMETHING I LEARNED THERE?

MY TOP THREE FAVORITE ACTIVITIES WERE . . .

1.

2.

3

MY TRIP WAS

/10

JAN   FEB   MAR   APR   MAY   JUN   JUL   AUG   SEP   OCT   NOV   DEC
1 2 3 4 5 6 7 8 9 10 11 12 13 14 15 16 17 18 19 20 21 22 23 24 25 26 27 28 29 30 31

....

....

....

....

....

....

....

....

....

....

....

....

....

....

....

....

....

....

....

....

....

....

....

HALEAKALĀ

HAWAI'I

 VISITORS CENTERS: Haleakalā Visitor Center I Kīpahulu Visitor Center I Park Headquarters Visitor Center

WHEN TO GO: The park is open year-round, 24 hours a day, and the temperatures range from 30°F to 65°F.

LODGING: Backcountry camping (permit required) I Two campgrounds (tents) I Wilderness cabins

---

HIKES:

Easy: Hōlua Cabin Trail I Hosmer Grove Loop I Leleiwi Overlook Trail I 'Ohe'o Gulch Trail I Pīpīwai Trail I Silversword Loop
Moderate: Ko'olau Gap Trail I Supply Trail I Waimoku Falls
Difficult: Haleakalā Crater Loop I Halemau'u Haleakalā Overlook Trail I Kaupo Trail I Keonehe'ehe'e (Sliding Sands) Trail I Kapalaoa Cabin Trail

ACTIVITIES:

Bird-watching I Hana Highway I 'Īao Valley State Park I Kanaha Pond Wildlife Sanctuary I Keālia Pond National Wildlife Refuge I Kīpahulu Biological Reserve I Polipoli Spring State Recreation Area I Wai'anapanapa State Park I Waikamoi Preserve

WILDLIFE SPOTTING:

Ākohekohe I 'Alauahio I 'Amakihi I 'Apapane I Green sea turtles I Haleakalā flightless moths I Hawaiian hoary bats I Hawaiian monk seals I Hawaiian wolf spiders I 'I'iwi I Kiwikiu I Nalo meli maoli I Nananana makaki'i I Nēnē I Pueo I 'Ua'u

---

DATE VISITED:

WEATHER:

WHERE I WENT:

WHERE I STAYED:

WHO I WENT WITH:

FAVORITE MOMENT:

WHAT I'D RECOMMEND:

TIPS TO FRIENDS/ FAMILY:

WHAT I WISH I KNEW BEFORE GOING:

WHAT WAS THE FIRST THING I NOTICED WHEN I ARRIVED?

MY FAVORITE PART OF THE VISIT WAS . . .

HOW I SPENT MY TIME THERE:

WHAT WOULD I DO IF I GO BACK?

WHAT IS SOMETHING I LEARNED THERE?

MY TOP THREE FAVORITE ACTIVITIES WERE . . .

1.

2.

3

MY TRIP WAS

/10

JAN   FEB   MAR   APR   MAY   JUN   JUL   AUG   SEP   OCT   NOV   DEC
1 2 3 4 5 6 7 8 9 10 11 12 13 14 15 16 17 18 19 20 21 22 23 24 25 26 27 28 29 30 31

HAWAI'I VOLCANOES

HAWAI'I

HAWAI'I VOLCANOES EST 1916

VISITORS CENTER: Kilauea Visitor Center

WHEN TO GO: The park is open year-round; summer and the winter holidays are typically the busiest seasons.

LODGING: Two campgrounds (tents, cabins) I Volcano House (rooms)

HIKES:

Easy: Devastation Trail I Ha'akulamanu Trail I Kau Desert Footprints Trail I Palm Trail I Pit Crater I Pu'u Huluhulu Trail I Pu'uloa Petroglyphs Trail I Pu'u o Lokuana Loop I Steaming Bluff I Thurston Lava Tube Trail

Moderate: Crater Rim Trail I Halema'uma'u Trail I Iliahi Trail I Kīlauea Iki Trail I Kahuku Forest Trail I Kona Trail I Nāulu Trail I Old Hawaiian Trail

Difficult: Halapē Trail I Hilina Pali Trail I Ka'aha Trail I Keauhou Trail I Mauna Loa Trail I Observatory Trail I Puna Kau Trail I Summit Trail

ACTIVITIES:

Bird-watching I Chain of Craters Road I Crater Rim Drive I Climbing on old lava flows I Hilina Pali Overlook I Hōlei Sea Arch I Kahuku Unit I Halema'uma'u Crater I Mauna Loa Road

WILDLIFE SPOTTING:

'Akiapōlā'au I 'Alalā I 'Apapane I Green sea turtles I Hawai'i 'ākepa I Hawai'i 'amakihi I Hawai'i creepers I Hawai'i 'elepaio I Hawaiian hoary bats I Hawaiian honeycreepers I Hawaiian monk seals I Hawksbill turtles I Humpback whales I 'I'iwi I 'Io I Kamehameha butterflies I Koa'e kea I Nēnē I 'Ōma'o I 'Ua'u

---

DATE VISITED:

WEATHER:

WHERE I WENT:

WHERE I STAYED:

WHO I WENT WITH:

FAVORITE MOMENT:

WHAT I'D RECOMMEND:

TIPS TO FRIENDS/ FAMILY:

WHAT I WISH I KNEW BEFORE GOING:

WHAT WAS THE FIRST THING I NOTICED WHEN I ARRIVED?

MY FAVORITE PART OF THE VISIT WAS . . .

HOW I SPENT MY TIME THERE:

WHAT WOULD I DO IF I GO BACK?

WHAT IS SOMETHING I LEARNED THERE?

MY TOP THREE FAVORITE ACTIVITIES WERE . . .

1.

2.

3

MY TRIP WAS

/10

JAN   FEB   MAR   APR   MAY   JUN   JUL   AUG   SEP   OCT   NOV   DEC
1 2 3 4 5 6 7 8 9 10 11 12 13 14 15 16 17 18 19 20 21 22 23 24 25 26 27 28 29 30 31

....

....

....

....

....

....

....

....

....

....

....

....

....

....

....

....

....

....

....

....

....

....

....

JOSHUA TREE

CALIFORNIA

VISITORS CENTERS: Black Rock Nature Center I Cottonwood Visitor Center I Joshua Tree Visitor Center

WHEN TO GO: Spring and fall are the most popular times to visit. Spring temperatures are particularly nice, summer can be exceptionally hot, and winter can be chilly.

LODGING: Eight campgrounds (tents, RVs, horse trailers)

HIKES:

Easy: Arch Rock Trail I Barker Dam Trail I Black Rock Canyon Trail I Cottonwood Spring Oasis I Covington Crest Trail I Desert Queen Mine Trail I Hidden Valley I Ryan Ranch I Split Rock Loop Trail I Wall Street Mill I Warren Peak Trail I Willow Hole
Moderate: Big Pine Trail I Burnt Hill Trail I Eagle Cliff Mine I Fortynine Palms Oasis Trail I Inspiration Peak Trail I Keys View Trail I Lost Horse Loop I Lost Palms Oasis I Maze Loop I Panorama Loop I Pine City Trail I Ryan Mountain I Silver Bell Mine
Difficult: Boy Scout Trail I Pinkham Canyon Road I Rattlesnake Canyon

ACTIVITIES:

Barker Dam I Cholla Cactus Garden I Geology Tour Road (4WD required) I Hall of Horrors rock climbing I Jumbo Rocks I Keys Ranch (reservation required) I Lost Horse Valley I Oyster Bar rock climbing I Park Boulevard I Pinto Basin Road I Skull Rock

WILDLIFE SPOTTING:

American badgers I Big brown bats I Bighorn sheep I Black-tailed jackrabbits I Bobcats I Coyotes I Desert kit foxes I Desert tortoises I Gophers I Kangaroo rats I Long-tailed weasels I Mountain lions I Mule deer I Rattlesnakes I Ringtails I Western yellow bats

DATE VISITED:

WEATHER:

WHERE I WENT:

WHERE I STAYED:

WHO I WENT WITH:

FAVORITE MOMENT:

WHAT I'D RECOMMEND:

TIPS TO FRIENDS/ FAMILY:

WHAT I WISH I KNEW BEFORE GOING:

WHAT WAS THE FIRST THING I NOTICED WHEN I ARRIVED?

MY FAVORITE PART OF THE VISIT WAS . . .

HOW I SPENT MY TIME THERE:

WHAT WOULD I DO IF I GO BACK?

WHAT IS SOMETHING I LEARNED THERE?

MY TOP THREE FAVORITE ACTIVITIES WERE . . .

1.

2.

3

MY TRIP WAS

/10

JAN   FEB   MAR   APR   MAY   JUN   JUL   AUG   SEP   OCT   NOV   DEC
1 2 3 4 5 6 7 8 9 10 11 12 13 14 15 16 17 18 19 20 21 22 23 24 25 26 27 28 29 30 31

....

....

....

....

....

....

....

....

....

....

....

....

....

....

....

....

....

....

....

....

....

....

....

PINNACLES

CALIFORNIA

 **VISITORS CENTERS:** Pinnacles Visitor Center I West Pinnacles Visitor Contact Station

WHEN TO GO: Mid-February to early June is the most ideal time to visit the park, as wildflowers are in bloom and the heat isn't as intense. Summer through early fall is very hot and dry.

LODGING: One campground (tents, RVs)

HIKES:
Easy: Bear Gulch Cave Trail I Jawbone Trail I Prewett Point Trail
Moderate: Balconies Cave Trail I Balconies Cliffs-Cave Loop Trail I Bench Trail I Chalone Peak Trail I Moses Spring-Rim Trail Loop I Old Pinnacles Loop Trail I South Wilderness Trail
Difficult: Condor Gulch-High Peaks Loop Trail I High Peaks Trail I Juniper Canyon Trail I North Wilderness Trail

ACTIVITIES:
Bear Gulch Nature Center I Bird-watching I Exploring Talus Cave (Balconies Cave and Bear Gulch Cave) I Ranger-led programs I Rock climbing I Swimming at the campground pool I Wildflower blooms

WILDLIFE SPOTTING:
Alligator lizards I Badgers I Big brown bats I Bobcats I Brush rabbits I California condors I Coyotes I Gilbert's skinks I Ground squirrels I Jackrabbits I Merriam's chipmunks I Red-legged frogs I Striped racers I Townsend's big-eared bats I Western fence lizards I Western mastiff bats I Western red bats

DATE VISITED:

WEATHER:

WHERE I WENT:

WHERE I STAYED:

WHO I WENT WITH:

FAVORITE MOMENT:

WHAT I'D RECOMMEND:

TIPS TO FRIENDS/ FAMILY:

WHAT I WISH I KNEW BEFORE GOING:

WHAT WAS THE FIRST THING I NOTICED WHEN I ARRIVED?

MY FAVORITE PART OF THE VISIT WAS . . .

HOW I SPENT MY TIME THERE:

WHAT WOULD I DO IF I GO BACK?

WHAT IS SOMETHING I LEARNED THERE?

MY TOP THREE FAVORITE ACTIVITIES WERE . . .

1.

2.

3

MY TRIP WAS

/10

JAN   FEB   MAR   APR   MAY   JUN   JUL   AUG   SEP   OCT   NOV   DEC
1 2 3 4 5 6 7 8 9 10 11 12 13 14 15 16 17 18 19 20 21 22 23 24 25 26 27 28 29 30 31

....

....

....

....

....

....

....

....

....

....

....

....

....

....

....

....

....

....

....

....

....

....

....

SEQUOIA & KINGS CANYON

CALIFORNIA

SEQUOIA & KINGS CANYON
1890/1940

VISITORS CENTERS (SEQUOIA): Foothills Visitor Center I Giant Forest Museum I Lodgepole Visitor Center I Mineral King Ranger Station **(KINGS CANYON):** Cedar Grove Visitor Center I Kings Canyon Visitor Center

WHEN TO GO: Both parks are open year-round; summer is the busiest season. Some of the main roads close during the winter.

LODGING (SEQUOIA): Nine campgrounds (tents, RVs) I Wuksachi Lodge **(KINGS CANYON):** Five campgrounds (tent, RVs) I Cedar Grove Lodge I Grant Grove Cabins I John Muir Lodge

---

HIKES:
Easy: Big Stump Loop Trail I Big Trees Trail I Congress Trail I Crescent Meadow Loop I General Grant Tree Trail I Hanging Rock Trail I Hazelwood Nature Loop I North Grove Loop Trail I Paradise Creek Trail I Roaring River Falls I Tharp's Log Trail I Zumwalt Meadow
Moderate: Big Baldy Ridge I Buena Vista Trail I Ella Falls Loop I Ladybug Trail I Little Baldy Trail I Marble Falls Trail I Mist Falls I Moro Rock I Muir Grove Trail I Sequoia Lake Trail I Sugar Pine Trail I Timber Gap I Tokopah Falls I Viola Falls I Watchtower Trail
Difficult: Bubbs Creek Trail I Eagle Lake Trail I Franklin Lakes I High Sierra Trail I Lakes Trail I Middle Fork Trail I Monarch Lakes Trail I Mosquito Lakes I Mount Baldy I Paradise Valley Trail I Sawtooth Pass Trail I Twin Lakes Trail I White Chief Trail

ACTIVITIES:
Crystal Cave Tour I Generals Highway I General Sherman Tree I Giant Forest Museum I Grant Grove Village I Hospital Rock I Kings Canyon Scenic Byway I Mineral King Drive I Climbing Moro Rock I Wuksachi Village

WILDLIFE SPOTTING:
Acorn woodpeckers I Black bears I Bobcats I California kingsnakes I California newts I California quails I Gopher snakes I Lesser goldfinches I Pocket gophers I Scrub jays I Spotted skunks I Striped racers I Striped skunks I Western whiptail lizards I Wood rats I Wrentits

---

DATE VISITED:

WEATHER:

WHERE I WENT:

WHERE I STAYED:

WHO I WENT WITH:

FAVORITE MOMENT:

WHAT I'D RECOMMEND:

TIPS TO FRIENDS/ FAMILY:

WHAT I WISH I KNEW BEFORE GOING:

WHAT WAS THE FIRST THING I NOTICED WHEN I ARRIVED?

MY FAVORITE PART OF THE VISIT WAS . . .

HOW I SPENT MY TIME THERE:

WHAT WOULD I DO IF I GO BACK?

WHAT IS SOMETHING I LEARNED THERE?

MY TOP THREE FAVORITE ACTIVITIES WERE . . .

1.

2.

3

MY TRIP WAS

/10

JAN   FEB   MAR   APR   MAY   JUN   JUL   AUG   SEP   OCT   NOV   DEC
1 2 3 4 5 6 7 8 9 10 11 12 13 14 15 16 17 18 19 20 21 22 23 24 25 26 27 28 29 30 31

YOSEMITE

CALIFORNIA

VISITORS CENTERS: Big Oak Flat Welcome Center I Happy Isles Art and Nature Center I Tuolumne Meadows Visitor Center I Yosemite Valley Visitor Center I Wawona Visitor Center

WHEN TO GO: The park is open year-round, but some roads might be closed from November to May, depending on weather. Late spring, summer, and early fall are the busiest seasons.

LODGING: Thirteen campgrounds (tents, RVs, camper vans, horse trailers)

HIKES:

Easy: Bridalveil Fall Trail I Cook's Meadow I East Valley Loop Trail I Glacier Point Trail I Lower Yosemite Fall Trail I Mirror Lake Trail I Olmsted Point Nature Trail I Swinging Bridge Trail I Valley Floor Loop Trail I West Valley Loop Trail

Moderate: Artist Point Trail I Cathedral Lakes Trail I Dewey Point Trail Loop I Inspiration Point Trail I Lembert Dome Loop I Lower Chilnualna Falls Trail I May Lake Trail I Nevada Falls Trail I Rancheria Falls Trail I Sentinel Dome Trail I Tenaya Lake Loop I Wapama Falls Trail

Difficult: Clouds Rest Trail I Eagle Peak I El Capitan Loop I Four Mile Trail I Half Dome Trail I John Muir Trail I Little Yosemite Valley Trail I Mount Hoffman Trail I North Dome Trail I Panorama Trail I Sunrise Lakes I Ten Lakes Trail I Upper Yosemite Falls

ACTIVITIES:

Ansel Adams Gallery I El Capitan climb I Glacier Point Road I Hetch Hetchy drive I Indian Village of Ahwahnee I Pioneer Yosemite History Center I Tioga Road I Wawona Tunnel Tree I Wilderness Center I Yosemite Village I Yosemite Museum

WILDLIFE SPOTTING:

American dippers I Black bears I California ground squirrels I California spotted owls I Coast horned lizards I Coyotes I Douglas squirrels I Eastern kingbirds I Mountain chickadees I Mountain lions I Mule deer I Pacific fishers I Sierra fence lizards I Sierra garter snakes I Sierra Nevada bighorn sheep I Sierra Nevada red foxes I Western pond turtles I Western tanagers I Woodchucks I Yellow-bellied marmots

---

DATE VISITED:

WEATHER:

WHERE I WENT:

WHERE I STAYED:

WHO I WENT WITH:

FAVORITE MOMENT:

WHAT I'D RECOMMEND:

TIPS TO FRIENDS/ FAMILY:

WHAT I WISH I KNEW BEFORE GOING:

WHAT WAS THE FIRST THING I NOTICED WHEN I ARRIVED?

MY FAVORITE PART OF THE VISIT WAS . . .

HOW I SPENT MY TIME THERE:

WHAT WOULD I DO IF I GO BACK?

WHAT IS SOMETHING I LEARNED THERE?

MY TOP THREE FAVORITE ACTIVITIES WERE . . .

1.

2.

3

MY TRIP WAS

/10

JAN   FEB   MAR   APR   MAY   JUN   JUL   AUG   SEP   OCT   NOV   DEC
1   2   3   4   5   6   7   8   9   10   11   12   13   14   15   16   17   18   19   20   21   22   23   24   25   26   27   28   29   30   31

....

....

....

....

....

....

....

....

....

....

....

....

....

....

....

....

....

....

....

....

....

....

....

CRATER LAKE

OREGON

 **VISITORS CENTERS:** Rim Visitor Center I Steel Visitor Center

 **WHEN TO GO:** Winter comes early and lingers, so most roads aren't clear until late June or early July. Rim Village remains open year-round for winter recreational activities.

 **LODGING:** Backcountry camping (permit required) I Two campgrounds (tents, RVs) I Cabins at Mazama Village I Crater Lake Lodge

---

• HIKES:

Easy: Castle Crest Wildflower Trail I Discovery Point Trail I Fumarole Bay Trail I Godfrey Glen Trail I Lady of the Woods Trail I Pinnacles Valley Trail I Plaikni Falls Trail I Sun Notch Trail

Moderate: Annie Creek Canyon Trail I Cleetwood Cove Trail I Crater Peak Trail I Dutton Creek Trail I Garfield Peak Trail I Lightning Spring Trail I Mount Scott Trail I Raven Trail I Stuart Falls Trail I Union Peak Trail I Watchman Peak Trail I Wizard Island Trail

Difficult: Hillman Peak I Pacific Crest Trail and Alternate Loop

• ACTIVITIES:

Crater Lake Boat Tours I Crater Lake Rim Scenic Drive I Klamath Marsh National Wildlife Refuge I Newberry National Volcanic Monument I Oregon Caves National Monument I Oregon Dunes National Recreation Area I Prospect State Scenic Viewpoint I Rogue Wild and Scenic River I Wizard Island Tours

• WILDLIFE SPOTTING:

American dippers I American martens I Black-backed woodpeckers I Black bears I Bobcats I Cascades frogs I Clark's nutcrackers I Coyotes I Douglas squirrels I Gray-crowned rosyfinches I Long-toed salamanders I Mazama newts I Mountain bluebirds I Pacific tree frogs I Pikas I Red foxes I Snowshoe hares I Striped skunks

---

DATE VISITED:

WEATHER:

WHERE I WENT:

WHERE I STAYED:

WHO I WENT WITH:

FAVORITE MOMENT:

WHAT I'D RECOMMEND:

TIPS TO FRIENDS/ FAMILY:

WHAT I WISH I KNEW BEFORE GOING:

WHAT WAS THE FIRST THING I NOTICED WHEN I ARRIVED?

MY FAVORITE PART OF THE VISIT WAS . . .

HOW I SPENT MY TIME THERE:

WHAT WOULD I DO IF I GO BACK?

WHAT IS SOMETHING NEW I LEARNED?

MY TOP THREE FAVORITE ACTIVITIES WERE . . .

1.

2.

3

MY TRIP WAS

JAN   FEB   MAR   APR   MAY   JUN   JUL   AUG   SEP   OCT   NOV   DEC
1 2 3 4 5 6 7 8 9 10 11 12 13 14 15 16 17 18 19 20 21 22 23 24 25 26 27 28 29 30 31

....

....

....

....

....

....

....

....

....

....

....

....

....

....

....

....

....

....

....

....

....

....

....

LASSEN VOLCANIC

CALIFORNIA

VISITORS CENTER: Kohm Yah-mah-nee Visitor Center

WHEN TO GO: The park is open year-round, but many facilities are closed from mid-October to late May. The main park highway is also closed during the winter season.

LODGING: Backcountry camping (permit required) I Seven campgrounds (tents, RVs, campers) I Drakesbad Guest Ranch

---

HIKES:

Easy: Bathtub Lake Trail I Boiling Springs Lake Trail I Bumpass Hell Trail I Devastated Area Interpretive Trail I Dream Lake Trail I Lily Pond Nature Trail I Manzanita Lake Loop I Reflection Lake Trail I Shadow Lake Trail I Sulphur Works

Moderate: Cold Boiling Lake Trail I Crags Lake Trail I Crystal Lake Trail I Devils Kitchen Trail I Diamond Peak Trail I Drake Lake Trail I Echo Lake Trail I Forest Lake Trail I Inspiration Point Trail I Juniper Lake Loop I Kings Creek Falls Trail I Manzanita Creek Trail I Mount Harkness Loop Trail I Rainbow Lake Trail I Ridge Lakes Trail I Sifford Lakes Trail

Difficult: Brokeoff Mountain Trail I Butte Lake Loop I Cinder Cone Trail I Lassen Peak Trail I Prospect Peak Trail I Nobles Emigrant Trail

ACTIVITIES:

Drakesbad Guest Ranch I Fantastic Lava Beds I Fishing I Lassen Volcanic National Park Highway I Loomis Museum I Paddling at Manzanita Lake I Ranger-led programs I Warner Valley

WILDLIFE SPOTTING:

American badgers I American martens I American robins I Anna's hummingbirds I Big brown bats I Black bears I Bobcats I Clark's nutcrackers I Coyotes I Douglas squirrels I Fishers I Golden-crowned kinglets I Great gray owls I Mountain chickadees I Mountain lions I Mule deer I Muskrats I Ospreys I Pikas I Pileated woodpeckers I Red foxes I Snowshoe hares I Steller's jays I Striped skunks I Yellow-rumped warblers

---

DATE VISITED:

WEATHER:

WHERE I WENT:

WHERE I STAYED:

WHO I WENT WITH:

FAVORITE MOMENT:

WHAT I'D RECOMMEND:

TIPS TO FRIENDS/ FAMILY:

WHAT I WISH I KNEW BEFORE GOING:

WHAT WAS THE FIRST THING I NOTICED WHEN I ARRIVED?

MY FAVORITE PART OF THE VISIT WAS . . .

HOW I SPENT MY TIME THERE:

WHAT WOULD I DO IF I GO BACK?

WHAT IS SOMETHING NEW I LEARNED?

MY TOP THREE FAVORITE ACTIVITIES WERE . . .

1.

2.

3

MY TRIP WAS

/10

JAN   FEB   MAR   APR   MAY   JUN   JUL   AUG   SEP   OCT   NOV   DEC
1 2 3 4 5 6 7 8 9 10 11 12 13 14 15 16 17 18 19 20 21 22 23 24 25 26 27 28 29 30 31

MOUNT RAINIER

WASHINGTON

 VISITORS CENTERS: Henry M. Jackson Memorial Visitor Center I Longmire Wilderness Information Center I Ohanapecosh Visitor Center I Sunrise Visitor Center

WHEN TO GO: Nisqually Entrance to Paradise is open year-round, but most other roads into the park are closed from mid-November to June or July. Crowds and wildflowers peak in early August.

LODGING: Three campgrounds (tents, RVs) I National Park Inn I Paradise Inn

---

- **HIKES:**

Easy: Box Canyon Trail I Naches Peak Loop Trail I Nisqually Vista Trail I Reflection Lakes Loop I Silver Falls Trail I Sunrise Nature Trail I Tipsoo Lake Loop I Trail of the Shadows
Moderate: Bench and Snow Lakes Trail I Carbon Glacier Trail I Dewey Lake Trail I Glacier Basin Trail I Golden Gate Trail I Dege Peak Trail I Green Lake Trail I Grove of the Patriarchs Trail I Narada Falls Trail I Old Mine Trail I Paradise Glacier Trail I Spray Park Trail to Mount Pleasant I Tolmie Peak Lookout Trail
Difficult: Alta Vista Trail I Burroughs Mountain Loop Trail I Crystal Peak Trail I Mount Rainier Standard Summit Route I Pinnacle Peak Trail I Skyline Trail

- **ACTIVITIES:**

Biking I Cross-country skiing or snowshoeing I Fishing I Longmire Museum I Mount Rainier Valor Memorial I Rock climbing I Walking tours in Longmire

- **WILDLIFE SPOTTING:**

American martens I American mink I Black bears I Columbian black-tailed deer I Coyotes I Elk I Hoary marmots I Kingfishers I Long-tailed weasels I Moose I Mountain goats I Mountain lions I Mule deer I Pikas I Red foxes I Snowshoe hares I Striped skunks I Wolverines

---

DATE VISITED:

WEATHER:

WHERE I WENT:

WHERE I STAYED:

WHO I WENT WITH:

FAVORITE MOMENT:

WHAT I'D RECOMMEND:

TIPS TO FRIENDS/ FAMILY:

WHAT I WISH I KNEW BEFORE GOING:

WHAT WAS THE FIRST THING I NOTICED WHEN I ARRIVED?

MY FAVORITE PART OF THE VISIT WAS . . .

HOW I SPENT MY TIME THERE:

WHAT WOULD I DO IF I GO BACK?

WHAT IS SOMETHING NEW I LEARNED?

MY TOP THREE FAVORITE ACTIVITIES WERE . . .

1.

2.

3

MY TRIP WAS

/10

NORTH CASCADES

WASHINGTON

NORTH CASCADES EST 1968

VISITORS CENTERS: Golden West Visitor Center I North Cascades Visitor Center I North Cascades Wilderness Information Center I Park and Forest Information Center

WHEN TO GO: Park roads close in the winter, but ferries run year-round. Backcountry trails start to clear in May; snow can linger into July.

LODGING: Six campgrounds (tents, RVs) I North Cascade Lodge I Ross Lake Resort I Silver Bay Inn & Resort I Stehekin Valley Ranch

HIKES:
Easy: Agnes Gorge Trail I Gorge Creek Falls Trail I Happy Creek Forest Walk I Rock Shelter Trail I Skagit River Loop Trail I Trail of the Cedars Nature Walk
Moderate: Cascade Pass Trail I Old Wagon Trail I Pacific Northwest Trail
Difficult: Bridge Creek Trail I Eldorado Peak I Forbidden Peak Trail I McGregor Mountain Trail I Pacific Crest Trail I Sourdough Mountain Lookout I Thunder Creek Trail

ACTIVITIES:
Buckner Homestead Historic District I Liberty Bell and Early Winters Spires climbing I Diablo Dam I Diablo Lake I Newhalem I Ross Lake National Recreation Area I Thunder Creek I Wilderness Information Center I Winthrop

WILDLIFE SPOTTING:
Black bears I Bobcats I Columbia black-tailed deer I Cougars I Elk I Flycatchers I Harlequin ducks I Hoary marmots I Lynx I Moose I Mountain goats I Ospreys I Pikas I Western small-footed bats

DATE VISITED:

WEATHER:

WHERE I WENT:

WHERE I STAYED:

WHO I WENT WITH:

FAVORITE MOMENT:

WHAT I'D RECOMMEND:

TIPS TO FRIENDS/ FAMILY:

WHAT I WISH I KNEW BEFORE GOING:

WHAT WAS THE FIRST THING I NOTICED WHEN I ARRIVED?

MY FAVORITE PART OF THE VISIT WAS . . .

HOW I SPENT MY TIME THERE:

WHAT WOULD I DO IF I GO BACK?

WHAT IS SOMETHING NEW I LEARNED?

MY TOP THREE FAVORITE ACTIVITIES WERE . . .

1.

2.

3

MY TRIP WAS

/10

JAN   FEB   MAR   APR   MAY   JUN   JUL   AUG   SEP   OCT   NOV   DEC

1 2 3 4 5 6 7 8 9 10 11 12 13 14 15 16 17 18 19 20 21 22 23 24 25 26 27 28 29 30 31

OLYMPIC

WASHINGTON

 **VISITORS CENTERS:** Hoh Rain Forest Visitor Center I Hurricane Ridge Visitor Center I Kalaloch Ranger Station I Olympic National Park Visitor Center

 **WHEN TO GO:** Activities are offered year-round in the park, even in the winter. Note: It can rain at any time in the westside rainforest.

LODGING: Five camp-grounds (tents, RVs, campers) I Kalaloch Lodge I Lake Crescent Lodge I Lake Quinault Lodge I Log Cabin Resort I Sol Duc Hot Springs Resort

HIKES:

Easy: Big Meadow Loop I Hall of Mosses Trail I Kalaloch Creek Nature Trail I Marymere Falls Trail I Ozette Loop I Quinault Rain Forest Nature Trail I Ruby Beach I Sand Point Trail I Second Beach Trail I Sol Duc Falls Trail I Spruce Nature Trail I Staircase Rapids Loop

Moderate: Cape Alava Trail I Deer Lake Trail I Dry Creek Trail I Hoh River Trail I Hurricane Hill via Hurricane Ridge I Olympic Hot Springs Trail I Ozette Triangle Trail I Peabody Creek Trail I Quinault River Pony Bridge Trail I Rialto Beach Trail I Wedding Rocks Trail I West Elwha River Trail

Difficult: Deer Ridge Trail I Flapjack Lakes Trail I Lake Angeles Trail I Mount Storm King I North Fork Skokomish River Trail I Olympic South Coast Trail I Pyramid Mountain Trail I Silver Lake Way Trail I Wagonwheel Lake Trail

ACTIVITIES:

Bird-watching and wildlife viewing I Boating on Lake Ozette I Canoeing or kayaking the Elwha River I Fishing I Visiting Forks I Driving Hurricane Ridge Road I Ranger-led programs I Skiing and snowshoeing at Hurricane Ridge I Stargazing I Tide pooling at Hole in the Wall

WILDLIFE SPOTTING:

Beavers I Black bears I Black-tailed deer I Bobcats I Gray whales I Mink I Muskrats I Olympic marmots I Puffins I River otters I Roosevelt elk I Sea lions I Seals I Spotted owls

---

DATE VISITED:

WEATHER:

WHERE I WENT:

WHERE I STAYED:

WHO I WENT WITH:

FAVORITE MOMENT:

WHAT I'D RECOMMEND:

TIPS TO FRIENDS/ FAMILY:

WHAT I WISH I KNEW BEFORE GOING:

WHAT WAS THE FIRST THING I NOTICED WHEN I ARRIVED?

MY FAVORITE PART OF THE VISIT WAS . . .

HOW I SPENT MY TIME THERE:

WHAT WOULD I DO IF I GO BACK?

WHAT IS SOMETHING NEW I LEARNED?

MY TOP THREE FAVORITE ACTIVITIES WERE . . .

1.

2.

3

MY TRIP WAS

/10

JAN   FEB   MAR   APR   MAY   JUN   JUL   AUG   SEP   OCT   NOV   DEC
1 2 3 4 5 6 7 8 9 10 11 12 13 14 15 16 17 18 19 20 21 22 23 24 25 26 27 28 29 30 31

....

....

....

....

....

....

....

....

....

....

....

....

....

....

....

....

....

....

....

....

....

REDWOOD

CALIFORNIA

VISITORS CENTERS: Crescent City Information Center I Hiouchi Visitor Center I Jedediah Smith Redwoods Visitor Center I Prairie Creek Visitor Center I Thomas H. Kuchel Visitor Center

WHEN TO GO: Crowded trails and bumper-to-bumper roads are seen during the summer, while spring is great for wildflowers, autumn has chromatic leaves, and winter means quieter groves.

LODGING: Backcountry camping (permit required) I Four campgrounds (tents, RVs)

- **HIKES:**

Easy: Ah-Pah Interpretive Trail I Farm Trail I Fern Canyon Loop Trail I Foothill Loop Trail I Lady Bird Johnson Grove Trail I Revelation Trail I Yurok Loop Trail
Moderate: Flint Ridge Section Trail I Hidden Beach Trail I Klamath River Overlook I McArthur Creek Loop I Ossagon Trail I Skunk Cabbage Trail I Tall Trees Grove Loop Trail I Trillium Falls Trail
Difficult: Bald Hills Road I Damnation Creek Trail I Mill Creek Horse Trail

- **ACTIVITIES:**

Biking I Big Tree Wayside I Bouldering I Jedediah Smith Redwoods State Park I National Tribute Grove I Newton B. Drury Scenic Parkway I Prairie Creek Redwoods State Park I Simpson-Reed Grove I Trees of Mystery

- **WILDLIFE SPOTTING:**

American beavers I American dippers I Bald eagles I Banana slugs I Big brown bats I Black-tailed deer I Bobcats I Brush rabbits I California brown pelicans I California sea lions I Chipmunks I Coyotes I Douglas squirrels I Giant green sea anemones I Gray foxes I Marbled murrelets I Mink I Mountain lions I Porcupines I Roosevelt elk I Salamanders I Striped skunks I Western meadowlarks

---

DATE VISITED:

WEATHER:

WHERE I WENT:

WHERE I STAYED:

WHO I WENT WITH:

FAVORITE MOMENT:

WHAT I'D RECOMMEND:

TIPS TO FRIENDS/ FAMILY:

WHAT I WISH I KNEW BEFORE GOING:

WHAT WAS THE FIRST THING I NOTICED WHEN I ARRIVED?

MY FAVORITE PART
OF THE VISIT WAS . . .

HOW I SPENT MY TIME THERE:

WHAT WOULD I DO IF I GO BACK?

WHAT IS SOMETHING
NEW I LEARNED?

MY TOP THREE FAVORITE ACTIVITIES WERE . . .

1.

2.

3

MY TRIP
WAS

/10

DENALI

ALASKA

 VISITORS CENTERS: Denali Visitor Center **I** Eielson Visitor Center **I** Murie Science and Learning Center **I** Walter Harper Talkeetna Ranger Station

WHEN TO GO: The park is open year-round. Summer solstice brings 21 hours of sunlight to Denali, and July usually offers the best weather.

LODGING: Backcountry camping (free permit required) **I** Six campgrounds (tents, RVs) **I** Camp Denali & North Face Lodge **I** Denali Backcountry Lodge **I** Kantishna Roadhouse **I** Skyline Lodge

---

HIKES:

Easy: Dragon Fly **I** Jonesville Trail **I** McKinley Station Trail **I** Morino Trail **I** Mountain Vista Loop Trail **I** Savage River Loop **I** Spruce Tree Trail **I** Riley Creek Trail **I** Roadside Trail **I** Tundra Loop Trail **I** Wonder Lake Trail

Moderate: Blueberry Hill Trail **I** Eldorado Creek Trail **I** Ermine Hill Trail **I** Gorge Creek Trail **I** Quigley Ridge Trail Loop **I** Primrose Ridge Trail **I** Rock Creek Trail **I** Taiga Trail

Difficult: Bison Gulch **I** Camp Ridge Trail **I** Mount Healy Overlook Trail **I** Savage Alpine Trail **I** Sugar Loaf Ridge

ACTIVITIES:

Bird-watching **I** Denali Park Road **I** Flightseeing **I** Kantishna mining community **I** Plains of Murie **I** Primrose Ridge **I** Savage River Bridge **I** Sled dog kennels **I** Teklanika River Bridge

WILDLIFE SPOTTING:

Arctic ground squirrels **I** Bald eagles **I** Black bears **I** Caribou **I** Dall sheep **I** Foxes **I** Golden eagles **I** Gray jays **I** Great horned owls **I** Grizzly bears **I** Lynx **I** Marmots **I** Mew gulls **I** Moose **I** Pikas **I** Red squirrels **I** Sharp-shinned hawks **I** Snowshoe hares **I** Wolves

---

DATE VISITED:

WEATHER:

WHERE I WENT:

WHERE I STAYED:

WHO I WENT WITH:

FAVORITE MOMENT:

WHAT I'D RECOMMEND:

TIPS TO FRIENDS/ FAMILY:

WHAT I WISH I KNEW BEFORE GOING:

WHAT WAS THE FIRST THING I NOTICED WHEN I ARRIVED?

MY FAVORITE PART OF THE VISIT WAS . . .

HOW I SPENT MY TIME THERE:

WHAT WOULD I DO IF I GO BACK?

WHAT IS SOMETHING NEW I LEARNED?

MY TOP THREE FAVORITE ACTIVITIES WERE . . .

1.

2.

3

MY TRIP WAS

GATES OF THE ARCTIC

ALASKA

 VISITORS CENTERS: Anaktuvuk Pass Ranger Station I Arctic Interagency Visitor Center I Fairbanks Alaska Public Lands Information Center I Gates of the Arctic Visitor Center

WHEN TO GO: While the winter is challenging and potentially dangerous, July and August are nearly perfect times to visit, and once the tundra is washed away, the autumn colors shine.

LODGING: Backcountry camping (no permit required; registering with the Park Service is highly recommended) I Bettles Lodge I Iniakuk Lake Wilderness Lodge I Peace of Selby Wilderness Lodge

---

HIKES:
There are no official trails, but visitors can hike throughout the park. However, hikers must be prepared for challenges. It is highly recommended to stop at a visitors center for general information and to attend a proper backcountry orientation that covers hiking basics and potential hazards of the area, including wildlife.

ACTIVITIES:
Anaktuvuk Pass day trips I Guided tours on the Noatak and Alatna Rivers I Cross-country skiing I Dog mushing I Flight-seeing Gates of the Arctic I Float trips on the Noatak I Houseboat stays on the Alatna River I Northern lights viewing I Paddling the Kobuk

WILDLIFE SPOTTING:
Arctic char I Beavers I Black bears I Brown bears I Canadian geese I Caribou I Chum salmon I Dall sheep I Dolly Varden trout I Falcons I Golden eagles I Graylings I Grizzly bears I Ground squirrels I Lemmings I Lynx I Moose I Musk oxen I Red foxes I Rough-legged hawks I Voles I Wolverines I Wolves

DATE VISITED:

WEATHER:

WHERE I WENT:

WHERE I STAYED:

WHO I WENT WITH:

FAVORITE MOMENT:

WHAT I'D RECOMMEND:

TIPS TO FRIENDS/ FAMILY:

WHAT I WISH I KNEW BEFORE GOING:

WHAT WAS THE FIRST THING I NOTICED WHEN I ARRIVED?

MY FAVORITE PART OF THE VISIT WAS . . .

HOW I SPENT MY TIME THERE:

WHAT WOULD I DO IF I GO BACK?

WHAT IS SOMETHING NEW I LEARNED?

MY TOP THREE FAVORITE ACTIVITIES WERE . . .

1.

2.

3

MY TRIP WAS

/10

GLACIER BAY

ALASKA

 VISITORS CENTERS: Glacier Bay National Park Visitor Center I Yakutat Ranger District Office

 **WHEN TO GO:** The park is most visited mid-May to mid-September; most services close the rest of the year.

LODGING: Backcountry camping (permit required) I One campground (tents) I Glacier Bay Lodge

---

HIKES:

Hiking is allowed throughout the park. However, hikers must be prepared for challenges. It is highly recommended to stop at a visitors center for general information and to attend a proper backcountry orientation that covers hiking basics and potential hazards of the area, including wildlife.

Easy: Bartlett River Trail I Forest Trail I Tlingit Trail
Moderate: Point Gustavus via Beach Trail
Difficult: Bartlett Lake Trail I Walker Glacier to Alsek River

ACTIVITIES:

Admiralty Island National Monument I Alaska Chilkat Bald Eagle Preserve I Bird-watching on South Marble Island I Private boat charters I Chilkat State Park I Glacier Bay Cruises I Excursions to Point Adolphus I Kayaking Bartlett Cove I Kayaking East Arm I Mendenhall Glacier I Misty Fjords National Monument I Russell Fjord Wilderness

WILDLIFE SPOTTING:

Cormorants I Grizzly bears I Harbor porpoises I Harbor seals I Humpback whales I Mountain goats I Murres I Pigeon guillemots I Puffins I Sea otters I Steller sea lions

---

DATE VISITED:

WEATHER:

WHERE I WENT:

WHERE I STAYED:

WHO I WENT WITH:

FAVORITE MOMENT:

WHAT I'D RECOMMEND:

TIPS TO FRIENDS/ FAMILY:

WHAT I WISH I KNEW BEFORE GOING:

WHAT WAS THE FIRST THING I NOTICED WHEN I ARRIVED?

MY FAVORITE PART OF THE VISIT WAS . . .

HOW I SPENT MY TIME THERE:

WHAT WOULD I DO IF I GO BACK?

WHAT IS SOMETHING NEW I LEARNED?

MY TOP THREE FAVORITE ACTIVITIES WERE . . .

1.

2.

3

MY TRIP WAS

/10

JAN   FEB   MAR   APR   MAY   JUN   JUL   AUG   SEP   OCT   NOV   DEC
1 2 3 4 5 6 7 8 9 10 11 12 13 14 15 16 17 18 19 20 21 22 23 24 25 26 27 28 29 30 31

....

....

....

....

....

....

....

....

....

....

....

....

....

....

....

....

....

....

....

....

....

....

....

KATMAI

ALASKA

 **VISITORS CENTERS:** Brooks Camp Visitor Center I King Salmon Visitor Center I Robert F. Griggs Visitor Center

 **WHEN TO GO:** For hiking, fishing, and boating, the best time to visit is June to mid-September. July, September, and October are peak bear-viewing months.

LODGING: Backcountry camping (no permit required; registering with the Park Service is highly recommended) I One campground (tents) I Brooks Lodge I Fure's Cabin I Grosvenor Lodge

HIKES:

Hiking is allowed throughout the park. However, hikers must be prepared for challenges. It is highly recommended to stop at a visitors center for general information and to attend a proper backcountry orientation that covers hiking basics and potential hazards of the area, including wildlife.

Easy: Brooks Falls Trail I Cultural Site Trail I Lake Brooks Road I Ukak Falls I Windy Creek Overlook
Moderate: Valley of Ten Thousand Smokes Road
Difficult: Dumpling Mountain Trail

ACTIVITIES:

Bay of Islands guided paddle tour I Bear viewing at Brooks Falls I Fure's Cabin I Guided floatplane for bear viewing I Paddling Savonoski Loop I Sightseeing tours I Fly-fishing on Brooks River I Valley of Ten Thousand Smokes tour

WILDLIFE SPOTTING:

Beavers I Beluga whales I Brown bears I Caribou I Gray whales I Gray wolves I Harbor seals I Humpback whales I Lynx I Martens I Mink I Moose I Orcas I Porcupines I Porpoises I Red foxes I River otters I Sea lions I Sea otters I Snowshoe hares I Weasels

---

DATE VISITED:

WEATHER:

WHERE I WENT:

WHERE I STAYED:

WHO I WENT WITH:

FAVORITE MOMENT:

WHAT I'D RECOMMEND:

TIPS TO FRIENDS/ FAMILY:

WHAT I WISH I KNEW BEFORE GOING:

WHAT WAS THE FIRST THING I NOTICED WHEN I ARRIVED?

MY FAVORITE PART OF THE VISIT WAS . . .

HOW I SPENT MY TIME THERE:

WHAT WOULD I DO IF I GO BACK?

WHAT IS SOMETHING NEW I LEARNED?

MY TOP THREE FAVORITE ACTIVITIES WERE . . .

1.

2.

3

MY TRIP WAS

/10

JAN   FEB   MAR   APR   MAY   JUN   JUL   AUG   SEP   OCT   NOV   DEC
1 2 3 4 5 6 7 8 9 10 11 12 13 14 15 16 17 18 19 20 21 22 23 24 25 26 27 28 29 30 31

KENAI FJORDS

ALASKA

 VISITORS CENTERS: Exit Glacier Nature Center **|** Kenai Fjords National Park Visitor Center

WHEN TO GO: The park is open year-round, but most visitors explore during the summer months, when boat trips are offered. Once there is enough snow coverage, the seven-mile road to Exit Glacier is open for all sorts of winter activities.

LODGING: Aialik and Holgate public use cabins (summer only) **|** Backcountry camping (no permit required; registering with the Park Service is highly recommended) **|** One campground (tents) **|** Kenai Fjords Glacier Lodge **|** Willow public use cabin

---

- **HIKES:**

Hiking is allowed throughout the park. However, hikers must be prepared for challenges. It is highly recommended to stop at a visitors center for general information and to attend a proper backcountry orientation that covers hiking basics and potential hazards of the area, including wildlife.
Easy: Glacier View Loop Trail **|** Rainforest Nature Walk
Moderate: Glacier Overlook Trail
Difficult: Harding Icefield Trail

- **ACTIVITIES:**

Aialik Bay Cabin **|** Cross-country skiing or snowmobiling Exit Glacier **|** Dogsledding **|** Enjoying excursions with commercial visitor services providers **|** Exploring fjords by boat **|** Tour Aialik Bay by floatplane **|** Holgate Cabin **|** Kayaking Kenai Fjords **|** Ranger-led walks **|** Resurrection Bay boat tour **|** Seward **|** Water taxiing to Bear Cove or McMullen Cove

- **WILDLIFE SPOTTING:**

Bald eagles **|** Black-billed magpies **|** Black oystercatchers **|** Brown bears **|** Dall's porpoises **|** Harbor porpoises **|** Harbor seals **|** Humpback whales **|** Marbled murrelets **|** Minke whales **|** Mountain goats **|** Orcas **|** Pacific white-sided dolphins **|** Puffins **|** Sea otters **|** Sei whales **|** Steller sea lions **|** Steller's jays

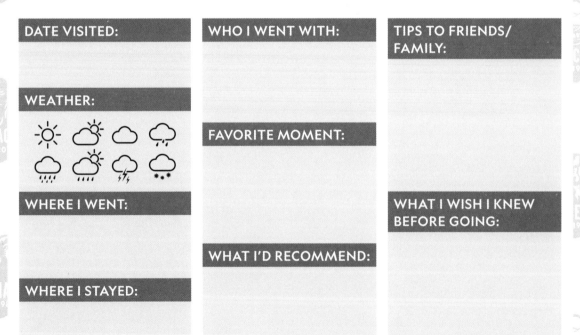

DATE VISITED:

WEATHER:

WHERE I WENT:

WHERE I STAYED:

WHO I WENT WITH:

FAVORITE MOMENT:

WHAT I'D RECOMMEND:

TIPS TO FRIENDS/ FAMILY:

WHAT I WISH I KNEW BEFORE GOING:

WHAT WAS THE FIRST THING I NOTICED WHEN I ARRIVED?

MY FAVORITE PART OF THE VISIT WAS . . .

HOW I SPENT MY TIME THERE:

WHAT WOULD I DO IF I GO BACK?

WHAT IS SOMETHING NEW I LEARNED?

MY TOP THREE FAVORITE ACTIVITIES WERE . . .

1.

2.

3

MY TRIP WAS

/10

JAN   FEB   MAR   APR   MAY   JUN   JUL   AUG   SEP   OCT   NOV   DEC
1 2 3 4 5 6 7 8 9 10 11 12 13 14 15 16 17 18 19 20 21 22 23 24 25 26 27 28 29 30 31

....

....

....

....

....

....

....

....

....

....

....

....

....

....

....

....

....

....

....

....

....

....

....

KOBUK VALLEY

ALASKA

 VISITORS CENTER: Northwest Arctic Heritage Center

 **WHEN TO GO:** The park is open year-round, but only very experienced wilderness adventurers should consider visiting outside summer months.

LODGING: Backcountry camping (no permit required for independent travelers; registering with the Park Service is highly recommended)

HIKES:

There are no official trails, but visitors can hike throughout the park. However, hikers must be prepared for challenges. It is highly recommended to stop at a visitors center for general information and to attend a proper backcountry orientation that covers hiking basics and potential hazards of the area, including wildlife.

ACTIVITIES:

Bering Land Bridge National Preserve I Great Kobuk Sand Dunes Hike I Kayaking the Kobuk River I Visiting Kotzebue I Noatak National Preserve I Onion Portage I Paddling the Salmon River I Privately operated canoe trips I Selawik National Wildlife Refuge I Wildlife-watching

WILDLIFE SPOTTING:

American wigeons I Black bears I Caribou I Foxes I Gray wolves I Grizzly bears I Moose I Musk oxen I Northern harriers I Pine grosbeaks I Plovers I Porcupines I Red-throated loons I River otters I Salmon I Wolverines

---

DATE VISITED:

WEATHER:

WHERE I WENT:

WHERE I STAYED:

WHO I WENT WITH:

FAVORITE MOMENT:

WHAT I'D RECOMMEND:

TIPS TO FRIENDS/ FAMILY:

WHAT I WISH I KNEW BEFORE GOING:

WHAT WAS THE FIRST THING I NOTICED WHEN I ARRIVED?

MY FAVORITE PART OF THE VISIT WAS . . .

HOW I SPENT MY TIME THERE:

WHAT WOULD I DO IF I GO BACK?

WHAT IS SOMETHING NEW I LEARNED?

MY TOP THREE FAVORITE ACTIVITIES WERE . . .

1.

2.

3

MY TRIP WAS

/10

JAN   FEB   MAR   APR   MAY   JUN   JUL   AUG   SEP   OCT   NOV   DEC

1 2 3 4 5 6 7 8 9 10 11 12 13 14 15 16 17 18 19 20 21 22 23 24 25 26 27 28 29 30 31

LAKE CLARK

ALASKA

VISITORS CENTER: Port Alsworth Visitor Center

WHEN TO GO: The park is open year-round, but the peak season runs from June through September, while June and July see the warmest weather, with temperatures between 50°F and 70°F.

LODGING: Accessible by floatplane or boat only I Backcountry camping (no permit required; registering with the Park Service is highly recommended) I Two campgrounds (tents) I Joe Thompson Cabin I Priest Rock Cabin

HIKES:

Hiking is allowed throughout the park. However, hikers must be prepared for challenges. It is highly recommended to stop at a visitors center for general information and to attend a proper backcountry orientation that covers hiking basics and potential hazards of the area, including wildlife.
Easy: Beaver Pond Loop I Tanalian Falls Trail I Telaquana Trail
Moderate: Eye of the Needle Viewpoint I Teetering Rock I Telaquana Route
Difficult: Portage Creek Trail I Tanalian Mountain Trail

ACTIVITIES:

Bear-watching at Chinitna Bay I Fishing Lake Clark I Fossil Point I Guided kayak adventures I Hnitsanghi'iy (Priest Rock) I Kijik National Historic Landmark I Richard Proenneke Cabin at Twin Lakes I Silver Salmon Creek guided fishing

WILDLIFE SPOTTING:

Arctic char I Arctic graylings I Arctic ground squirrels I Beavers I Black bears I Brown bears I Caribou I Dall sheep I Lynx I Moose I Peregrine falcons I Porcupines I Red foxes I Sharp-shinned hawks I Trout I Wolves

DATE VISITED:

WEATHER:

WHERE I WENT:

WHERE I STAYED:

WHO I WENT WITH:

FAVORITE MOMENT:

WHAT I'D RECOMMEND:

TIPS TO FRIENDS/ FAMILY:

WHAT I WISH I KNEW BEFORE GOING:

WHAT WAS THE FIRST THING I NOTICED WHEN I ARRIVED?

MY FAVORITE PART
OF THE VISIT WAS . . .

HOW I SPENT MY TIME THERE:

WHAT WOULD I DO IF I GO BACK?

WHAT IS SOMETHING
NEW I LEARNED?

MY TOP THREE FAVORITE ACTIVITIES WERE . . .

1.

2.

3

MY TRIP
WAS

/10

WRANGELL-ST. ELIAS

ALASKA

VISITORS CENTERS: Kennecott Visitor Center I Wrangell-St. Elias National Park Visitor Center

WHEN TO GO: The park is open year-round, but only experienced campers should explore outside of the summer months.

LODGING: Backcountry camping (except on private land, no permit required; registering with the Park Service is highly recommended) I Basic public use cabins I Kennicott Glacier Lodge

---

HIKES:

Hiking is allowed throughout the park. However, hikers must be prepared for challenges. It is highly recommended to stop at a visitors center for general information and to attend a proper backcountry orientation that covers hiking basics and potential hazards of the area, including wildlife.
Easy: Boreal Forest Loop I Valdez Trail I West Kennecott Glacier Trail
Moderate: Caribou Creek Trail I Copper Creek Trail to Copper Lake I Crystalline Hills Trail I McCarthy Creek Trail I Rambler Mine Trail I Skookum Volcano Trail
Difficult: Bonanza Mine Trail I Nabesna Road I Nugget Creek Trail I Root Glacier Trail I Soda Lake Trail I Suslota Lake Trail I The Goat Trail

ACTIVITIES:

Audio tours I Kennecott Mines National Historic Landmark I McCarthy Road I Nabesna Road I Rafting the Copper River Delta I Guided river tours I Root Glacier

WILDLIFE SPOTTING:

Beavers I Bison I Black bears I Brown bears I Caribou I Coyotes I Dall sheep I Grizzly bears I Ground squirrels I Harbor seals I Lynx I Marmots I Martens I Mountain goats I Pikas I Porcupines I Red foxes I River otters I Sea otters I Steller sea lions I Voles I Wolves

---

DATE VISITED:

WEATHER:

WHERE I WENT:

WHERE I STAYED:

WHO I WENT WITH:

FAVORITE MOMENT:

WHAT I'D RECOMMEND:

TIPS TO FRIENDS/ FAMILY:

WHAT I WISH I KNEW BEFORE GOING:

WHAT WAS THE FIRST THING I NOTICED WHEN I ARRIVED?

MY FAVORITE PART OF THE VISIT WAS . . .

HOW I SPENT MY TIME THERE:

WHAT WOULD I DO IF I GO BACK?

WHAT IS SOMETHING NEW I LEARNED?

MY TOP THREE FAVORITE ACTIVITIES WERE . . .

1.

2.

3

MY TRIP WAS

JAN   FEB   MAR   APR   MAY   JUN   JUL   AUG   SEP   OCT   NOV   DEC
1 2 3 4 5 6 7 8 9 10 11 12 13 14 15 16 17 18 19 20 21 22 23 24 25 26 27 28 29 30 31

....

....

....

....

....

....

....

....

....

....

....

....

....

....

....

....

....

....

....

....

....

....

NATIONAL PARK STAMPS

Collect your national park passport stamps here!

NATIONAL PARK STAMPS

Collect your national park passport stamps here!

NATIONAL PARK STAMPS

Collect your national park passport stamps here!

JAN   FEB   MAR   APR   MAY   JUN   JUL   AUG   SEP   OCT   NOV   DEC
1 2 3 4 5 6 7 8 9 10 11 12 13 14 15 16 17 18 19 20 21 22 23 24 25 26 27 28 29 30 31

JAN   FEB   MAR   APR   MAY   JUN   JUL   AUG   SEP   OCT   NOV   DEC

1   2   3   4   5   6   7   8   9   10   11   12   13   14   15   16   17   18   19   20   21   22   23   24   25   26   27   28   29   30   31

JAN   FEB   MAR   APR   MAY   JUN   JUL   AUG   SEP   OCT   NOV   DEC
1 2 3 4 5 6 7 8 9 10 11 12 13 14 15 16 17 18 19 20 21 22 23 24 25 26 27 28 29 30 31

JAN	FEB	MAR	APR	MAY	JUN	JUL	AUG	SEP	OCT	NOV	DEC

1 2 3 4 5 6 7 8 9 10 11 12 13 14 15 16 17 18 19 20 21 22 23 24 25 26 27 28 29 30 31

....

....

....

....

....

....

....

....

....

....

....

....

....

....

....

....

....

....

....

....

....

....

ILLUSTRATIONS CREDITS

All but one of the park icons seen throughout this journal were designed by Valerie Jar for the National Geographic National Parks app and are the property of the National Geographic Society. Anne LeongSon created the New River Gorge icon.

ACKNOWLEDGMENTS

Thank you to the team at National Geographic Books, especially Gabriela Capasso, for gathering all of this journal's useful information, and Anne LeongSon for its beautiful design. Also thank you to senior editor Allyson Johnson, editorial assistant Margo Rosenbaum, senior production editor Michael O'Connor, production editor Becca Saltzman, senior cartographer Mike McNey, senior cartographic research editor Michael J. Horner, and the entire team behind the original *National Geographic Guide to the National Parks*, 9th edition, the foundation of this journal.

National Geographic Partners, LLC
1145 17th Street NW
Washington, DC 20036-4688 USA

Get closer to National Geographic Explorers and photographers, and connect with our global community. Join us today at nationalgeographic.org/joinus

For rights or permissions inquiries, please contact National Geographic Books Subsidiary Rights: bookrights@natgeo.com

ISBN: 978-1-4262-2310-5

Printed in China
23/RRDH/1

The information in this book has been carefully checked and to the best of our knowledge is accurate. However, details are subject to change, and the publisher cannot be responsible for such changes, or for errors or omissions. Assessments of sites, lodging, and activities are based on the author's subjective opinions, which do not necessarily reflect the publisher's opinion.

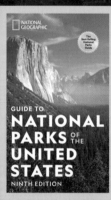